Personal Tax
(Finance Act 2024)

Tutorial

For assessments from 27 January 2025

Aubrey Penning
Bob Thomas

© Aubrey Penning, Bob Thomas, 2024.

All rights reserved. No part of this publication may be reproduced, stored in a retrieval system, or transmitted in any form or by any means, electronic, mechanical, photo-copying, recording or otherwise, without the prior consent of the copyright owners, or in accordance with the provisions of the Copyright, Designs and Patents Act 1988, or under the terms of any licence permitting limited copying issued by the Copyright Licensing Agency, Saffron House, 6-10 Kirby Street, London EC1N 8TS.

Published by Osborne Books Limited
Tel 01905 748071
Email books@osbornebooks.co.uk
Website www.osbornebooks.co.uk

Design by Laura Ingham

Printed by CPI Group (UK) Limited, Croydon, CR0 4YY, on environmentally friendly, acid-free paper from managed forests.

British Library Cataloguing in Publication Data
A catalogue record for this book is available from the British Library

ISBN 978-1-911681-12-0

Contents

Introduction

Tax data

1	Introduction to taxation	2
2	Income from property	32
3	Income from savings and investments	50
4	Income from employment	66
5	Preparing Income Tax computations	100
6	Capital Gains Tax	124
7	Inheritance Tax	158
	Answers to chapter activities	175
	AAT Reference Material	215
	Taxation tables	215
	Professional conduct in relation to taxation	223
	Index	242

Introduction

Qualifications covered

This book has been written specifically to cover the Unit 'Personal Tax' which is optional for the following qualifications:

AAT Level 4 Diploma in Professional Accounting

AAT Diploma in Professional Accounting – SCQF Level 8

The book contains a clear text with worked examples and case studies, chapter summaries and key terms to help with revision. Each chapter concludes with a wide range of activities, many in the style of AAT computer based assessments.

Osborne Study and Revision Materials

Additional materials, tailored to the needs of students studying this unit and revising for the assessment, include:

- **Workbooks:** paperback books with practice activities and exams
- **Student Zone:** access to Osborne Books online resources
- **Osborne Books App:** Osborne Books ebooks for mobiles and tablets

Visit www.osbornebooks.co.uk for details of study and revision resources and access to online material.

Exams, Finance Acts and tax years

This book has been designed to include guidance and exercises based on Tax Year 2024/25 (Finance Act 2024). We understand that the AAT plans to assess this legislation from 27 January 2025 to January 2026. Tutors and students are advised to check dates with the AAT and ensure that they sit the correct computer based assessment.

Tax data

INCOME TAX

Personal allowance £12,570
(subject to restrictions)

Personal savings allowance – basic rate taxpayers £1,000
 – higher rate taxpayers £500

Dividend allowance £500

Tax rates

	Basic rate	*Higher rate*	*Additional rate*
General Income	20%	40%	45%
Savings Income	20%	40%	45%
Dividend Income	*Dividend ordinary rate* 8.75%	*Dividend upper rate* 33.75%	*Dividend additional rate* 39.35%

Tax bands £

Basic rate/dividend ordinary rate to 37,700
Higher rate/dividend upper rate 37,701 – 125,140
Additional rate/dividend additional rate over 125,140

Company Car Benefit

g/km	% of list price
0 (e.g. pure electric)	2
1 – 50 (e.g. hybrid)	2 – 14 depending on electric only range
51 – 54	15
55 – 59	16
60 – 64	17

… and so on to a maximum of 37%

Diesel engine cars (except RDE2 compliant) add 4% to above

Company Car Fuel Benefit

Percentage for car (see company car benefit above) × £27,800

Authorised Mileage Rates (Mileage Allowance Payments – MAPs)

Cars and vans	First 10,000 miles in tax year	45p per mile
	Additional mileage	25p per mile
Motor cycles		24p per mile
Bicycles		20p per mile

NATIONAL INSURANCE CONTRIBUTIONS (NICS)

Employee's (primary) Class 1 rates:
    £242 – £967 per week   8%
    above £967 per week   2%

Employer's (secondary) Class 1 rates:
    above £175 per week   13.8%

Employer's Class 1A rates:
    all taxable benefits in kind   13.8%

CAPITAL GAINS TAX

Annual Exempt Amount

£3,000

CGT rate

Main rates   10% or 20%

1 Introduction to taxation

this chapter covers...

We start this chapter with an overview of the basic principles underlying taxation systems in general. We then go on to examine various tax structures and learn how to distinguish between progressive, proportional and regressive tax systems.

This is followed by a brief examination of the role of HMRC in the UK tax system and how law governs the way that tax is levied.

We then move on to start our study of Income Tax. We see how a basic computation is compiled and how income is divided up for tax purposes. The basis of assessment of the categories of income that we need to understand is also covered here, along with how tax bands work to calculate the total tax. The main forms of exempt income are also noted.

Next we look at the responsibilities of the taxpayer, including an understanding of tax planning, tax avoidance and tax evasion. This includes a summary of HMRC's approach to aggressive tax avoidance and the development of the 'General Anti Abuse Rule'.

The following section deals with the responsibilities of the tax practitioner, including what the AAT Code of Professional Ethics states.

The chapter is concluded with a section on residence and domicile that will help with understanding of the taxation of overseas income and gains.

TAX SYSTEMS

There are various taxes that apply in the UK. In this book we are going to examine Income Tax, Capital Gains Tax and Inheritance Tax. We will also see how National Insurance Contributions (which are also really a form of taxation) impact on employees and employers.

Before we start looking at the specifics of a particular tax we will take a step back so that we can look at the objectives and functions of taxation generally.

principles of taxation

The underlying premise of taxation is that it is the principal mechanism by which the state pays for the services and facilities that it provides for its citizens, and that all taxpayers should pay their fair contribution.

The principles of taxation are the basic concepts that can (or should) guide those who are developing a tax system. There are various principles that writers have proposed over the years.

As early as 1776, Adam Smith set out four principles in 'Wealth of Nations':

- burden proportionate to the ability to pay
- certainty
- convenience
- efficiency of collection

The main ideas in these principles continue to be used today, and will be referred to in the following list of principles, which is a combination of various current ideas.

- **Equity**

This is concerned with **fairness**, and links to the above idea of a proportionate tax burden. There are two main ways that equity can be considered.

The first is **horizontal equity** which means that individuals or businesses in the same situation (for example with the same income) should be treated in the same way (for example by having to pay the same amount of tax).

The second consideration is **vertical equity**. This is concerned that taxation is fair at different levels (for example different income levels) in society. In terms of taxes on income this would mean that those with higher income should pay a greater proportion of their income in tax. We will examine the issue of which tax structures achieve this a little later.

- **Simplicity**

This means that a tax system has rules which are clear and **understandable**. It includes the idea of **transparency** – so that there is no scope for discretion by tax officers about how much tax is due. This ties in with the principle of **certainty** listed above. Certainty can also be linked to the idea that tax rules should **not change retrospectively**. If a transaction has a particular tax implication when it is undertaken, then future tax laws should not change the position for that transaction.

- **Convenience**

Although most taxpayers would prefer not to pay tax at all, the method of collection must be convenient. For example, paying Income Tax through PAYE means that it is immediately deducted from the income to which it relates. Tax should not become due too long after the transactions that created the liability.

- **Stability**

Since decisions are made by organisations and individuals that have implications for many years, it is important that tax rules are stable, and do not change too radically or frequently. This means that taxation should be **predictable**, since that will help with long term planning.

- **Neutrality**

This idea is concerned that taxation rules should not unduly distort decisions that individuals and businesses undertake. Neutrality can help prevent unintended consequences of a taxation policy, as it minimises discrimination in favour of or against any particular economic choice. Some writers admit that all taxes result in behaviour changes and distortions, and that the tax system should be used to change behaviour to improve welfare and efficiency. An example of this is the taxation of tobacco products.

- **Efficiency and Effectiveness**

This principle states that costs of collection, administration and ensuring compliance should be minimised. Even at the extreme, these costs should not be greater than the amount of tax revenue generated. There can be a compromise here with the principle of convenience.

- **Flexibility**

Taxation systems should be able to keep pace with changes in technology and commerce. The impact of digital and global transactions represents a challenge for tax systems. Tax systems must also be able to respond to any future changes, which are difficult to predict. There must be a balance struck between flexibility and stability.

direct and indirect tax

Taxation can be divided into two types. Direct tax (for example Income Tax) is a tax which is levied on the income or profits of the person or organisation that pays it, rather than on goods or services. Indirect tax is charged on goods or services that consumers can choose whether to purchase. Although indirect tax is collected by intermediaries (for example retailers) it is ultimately borne by consumers. In the UK, Value Added Tax (VAT) is an example of an indirect tax.

tax structures

A tax structure is the combination of the tax base and the tax rates that are applied to the tax base.

The term **'tax base'** refers to the total income or assets that a tax can be applied to. For example, the tax base relating to Income Tax is the total taxable income of the population that the tax applies to. The tax threshold relating to Income Tax is the amount of income above which an individual begins to pay tax. This is determined by the personal allowance, as we will see later on. If the tax threshold is increased, then the tax base will be reduced, and if nothing else changes the total amount of tax raised will be reduced.

Tax rates apply to both direct and indirect taxes. The current Income Tax rates for general income are 20%, 40% and 45%, which apply to bands of taxable income. We will study how this Income Tax system works through Chapters 1 to 5 of this book.

progressive, proportional and regressive tax systems

These terms broadly describe how the amount of tax that is payable by individuals or organisations depends on their income or profits. This topic is closely related to the idea of equity (or fairness) that we described as a principle of taxation.

A **progressive** Income Tax system is one in which the lowest paid individuals pay the smallest proportion of their income in tax (or no tax at all), while the highest paid pay the largest proportion of their income in tax. The current UK Income Tax system is a progressive system. The following figures relate to taxable general income (after deducting the personal allowance). Different rules can apply to savings and dividend income, and the rules that apply to residents in Scotland are also different.

	Taxable income	
Basic rate band	£0 to £37,700	Charged at 20%
Higher rate band	£37,701 to £125,140	Charged at 40%
Additional rate band	over £125,140	Charged at 45%

Most individuals are entitled to a personal allowance which means that the first £12,570 of income per year is tax free.

The higher the individual's income, the more tax will be paid, both in total and as a proportion of their income.

For example, an individual with general income of £20,000 will pay no Income Tax on the first £12,570, and 20% on the rest, equalling (£7,430 x 20%) £1,486. This represents approximately 7% of their total income.

However, an individual with general income of £60,000 will pay Income Tax of £11,432. This is based on no Income Tax on the first £12,570, 20% on the next £37,700 and 40% on the rest. The tax of £11,432 represents approximately 19% of their total income.

If a tax is progressive, the **proportion** of total income that is paid in tax will rise throughout the range as **income increases**.

A **proportional** tax system applies the same rate of tax across the range. If an Income Tax system was proportional there would be no personal allowance and only one tax rate. Although those with higher incomes would pay more tax than those with a lower income, the tax as a proportion of income would be identical.

For example, if there was an Income Tax system with a single rate of 30% and no personal allowance, everyone would pay 30% of their income in tax.

An individual with income of £20,000 would pay £6,000 (30% of £20,000), and an individual with income of £60,000 would pay £18,000 (30% of £60,000). The amount of tax would be higher for higher incomes, but the **proportion** of income that is paid in tax would be the **same**.

Such a system would normally be considered unfair in comparison to a progressive tax system.

A **regressive** tax system is one where the proportion of income paid in tax **reduces** as income rises. Although a regressive Income Tax system would seem unlikely, there are some taxes that are regressive. National Insurance Contributions (NICs) for employees (that we will study later in this book) are regressive at some levels.

Employment earnings between £12,570 and £50,270 per year attract NI contributions of 8% of earnings within that band. Where earnings exceed £50,270 per year, the excess only attracts additional contributions of 2%.

For example, an employee earning **£40,000** per year would pay NIC of (£40,000 − £12,570) x 8% = £2,194. This equals about 5.5% of earnings.

However an employee earning **£80,000** per year would pay NIC of (£50,270 − £12,570) x 8% = £3,016, plus (£80,000 − £50,270) x 2% = £595. The NIC totals £3,611 which is equal to about 4.5% of earnings.

introduction to taxation

The above calculations are rounded for simplicity.

Employees with higher earnings than this would pay an even lower percentage of their earnings in NICs.

Some writers describe VAT as a regressive tax system since more VAT as a proportion of income is paid by those with lower incomes. This is because goods and services on which VAT is charged forms a larger part of the income of the less well off. As VAT is only incurred when money is spent, those with higher incomes pay less VAT as a proportion of income, as they tend to save (instead of spend) part of their earnings.

Any tax which is levied at a flat money amount can be considered regressive, since the amount is a lower proportion of the income of high earners. For example, if a UK television licence fee of £169.50 per year is thought of as a tax then its effect is regressive.

HM Revenue & Customs

In the UK, Income Tax, Capital Gains Tax, Inheritance Tax and National Insurance Contributions are all administered by the government department, formed by the amalgamation of the Inland Revenue and HM Customs & Excise. HM Revenue & Customs contains the following three parts:

- **taxpayer service offices** are the main offices that the taxpayer deals with and handle much of the basic Income Tax assessment and collection functions
- **taxpayer district offices** deal with more complex tax issues
- **tax enquiry centres** deal with enquiries and provide forms and leaflets to taxpayers

These three functions are located in offices throughout the UK. In smaller centres some functions may be combined into one office, while in larger towns and cities they may be located separately.

the law governing tax

The authority to impose taxes comes from two sources. The first is legislation passed by parliament, known as 'statute law'. You may have heard of the 'Finance Acts'. These are generally published each year and give details of any changes to taxes. These changes will have been proposed by the Chancellor of the Exchequer (usually in 'the budget') and passed by Parliament. In this book we will be using information from the Finance Act 2024, which relates to the tax year 2024/25. We will see exactly what is meant by tax years later in this chapter.

There are also other statute laws that were designed to create frameworks for the way that certain taxes work that continue to be relevant.

The second source of tax law is called 'case law', and arises from decisions taken in court cases. Taxation can be very complicated, and sometimes disagreements between HM Revenue & Customs and taxpayers result in court cases. The final outcome of such cases can then become 'case law' and influence future interpretation of statute law.

Although there is a substantial amount of both statute law and case law that governs the UK tax system, this book will try to keep references to specific law to a minimum. While it will be important to know the rules that apply to certain situations, you will not be required to quote from the legislation.

information available from HM Revenue & Customs

In addition to the tax law outlined above, there are interpretations and explanations of various issues that are published by HM Revenue & Customs. The main ones are as follows:

- extra-statutory concessions are issued by HM Revenue & Customs when they agree to impose a less strict interpretation of the law than would otherwise apply in particular circumstances

- HM Revenue & Customs statements of practice are public announcements of how the HMRC interprets specific rules

- Guides and Help Sheets are issued to help taxpayers complete the necessary return forms and calculate their tax

A large array of publications and forms can be downloaded from the Gov.uk website at www.gov.uk. It also provides data on rates and allowances for a range of tax years. You will find it useful to have a look at what is available on this site when you have an opportunity.

AN INTRODUCTION TO INCOME TAX

We will now start our study of one of the main taxes that are examined in this book – Income Tax. We briefly referred to the way that it works in our discussion of progressive tax systems.

The best way to start to understand how it works is to look at the 'Income Tax Computation' which will be based on a tax year.

An outline of an Income Tax computation is as follows:

	£
Income – both earnings and income from savings	X
less Personal allowance	(X)
Taxable Income	X
Tax payable on taxable income	X

A very simple Income Tax computation could be as follows:

	£
Income from earnings	20,000
less Personal Allowance	12,570
Taxable Income	7,430
Tax payable at 20%	1,486

Later in this chapter we will deal with Income Tax computations in more detail, but first we will consider some of the issues that might arise in computing Income Tax.

HOW INCOME IS DIVIDED UP FOR TAX PURPOSES

The income that an individual generates is divided into categories, depending on what sort of income it is and where it comes from. The categories are simply named after the type of income that they include. This is done so that:

- the correct rules on how to work out the income are used (since these vary with the categories), and
- the correct rates of tax are used (since they can also depend on the type of income)

the main categories of income

'Property Income'	Rental income from land and property.
'Trading Income'	Profits of trades and professions (the self-employed and those in partnership).
'Savings & Investment Income'	UK Interest and UK Dividends.
'Employment, pension and Social Security Income'	Income from employment etc. Income Tax is deducted from employment income under the system known as Pay-As-You-Earn (PAYE).

This list and descriptions have been simplified to include only the types of income that you need to know about. It does not include, for example, the categories that relate to overseas income.

tax years

For Income Tax purposes time is divided into 'tax years' (sometimes called 'fiscal years'). Individuals' income and Income Tax is worked out separately for each tax year. The tax year runs from 6 April in one calendar year to 5 April in the next calendar year. The tax year running from 6/4/24 to 5/4/25 would be described as the tax year 2024/25.

basis of assessment

As mentioned earlier, the income under each category will have different rules that determine how the income is worked out for tax purposes. The most important of these rules is known as the 'basis of assessment', and this simply considers whether the income assessable is the actual income receivable (the 'accruals' basis) or the income received in the tax year itself (the 'cash' basis). Later in the book we will look in more detail at the rules that govern each type of income. Here is a list of the main assessment rules for each category of income, with some comments about coverage in this book.

Property Income	**Rental income (after deducting allowable expenses) for the tax year, normally calculated on a cash basis.**
	We will look in more detail at rental income in Chapter 2.
Trading Income	**Profits (after deducting allowable expenses) for the tax year.**
	In this unit we only need to be aware that profits of the self-employed are included in the Income Tax calculations of individuals. The calculation of the profit for trading income is dealt with in the Business Tax unit.
Savings and Investment Income	**Gross interest received in the tax year. Amounts of dividends received in the tax year.**
	We will look in more detail at interest received and dividends in Chapter 3.
Employment, Pension and Social Security Income	**Amounts received in the tax year from employment etc, plus the value of any benefits, less any allowable deductions.**
	We will examine employment income in detail in Chapter 4.

HOW INCOME TAX IS CALCULATED

As already stated, Income Tax is usually worked out by using an 'Income Tax computation' for a specific tax year. This is a calculation that simply brings together the amounts of income from the various categories that apply to the individual and shows the workings for the tax that is payable. It is important that you are able to calculate an individual's Income Tax, so you will need to learn the basic computation structure and practise plenty of examples. The computation can be understood quite easily if we think of it as divided into three main parts.

1. The first part collects together and adds up the income from the different categories that are relevant. It is also a good idea to note in the computation any tax that has already been paid or deducted from each of these income sources, so that we can account for it later on. In complicated situations it will be necessary to calculate the income under each of the categories separately before the main computation is attempted.

2. The second part of the computation is where the personal allowance is deducted from the total income from the first section. Every individual (apart from those with very high income) has a personal allowance for each tax year. This represents the tax-free portion of their income for that year. The final figure that results from this section is known as the 'taxable income'.

3. The third part of the computation is where the taxable income from the previous part is used to calculate the amount of Income Tax. This is carried out using 'tax bands' and the percentage Income Tax rates that apply to each band. The total tax from this calculation is then compared with the amount already paid to arrive at the amount still owing to HM Revenue & Customs (or to the taxpayer). The final date for payment of Income Tax is 31 January following the end of the tax year.

Throughout this book we will use the allowances and tax bands relating to 2024/25. Whatever tax year is used, the principles and process are the same.

Full details of allowances and tax bands can be found at the beginning of this book. The majority of this data will also be provided in your examination. This AAT reference material is included as an appendix in this book.

personal allowance

The personal allowance is £12,570 for 2024/25. This is the amount that an individual's income can amount to in the tax year before they start paying Income Tax. It is always deducted from total income in the computation before the tax is calculated. Individuals with very high income (over £100,000) will have their personal allowances reduced or eliminated. We will see how this works in detail in Chapter 5. There are also separate allowances that relate specifically to savings income and dividends that apply to most people with this type of income. These allowances are in addition to the main personal allowances, and work in a slightly different way. We will examine how these allowances are used in detail in Chapter 3.

tax bands

The tax bands apply to an individual's taxable income – their total income for the year after the personal allowance has been deducted. The tax is calculated by multiplying the percentage shown by the income that falls into each band. This is done by starting with the lowest band and working up as far as necessary. The 2024/25 rates and bands are shown here:

Tax Bands for tax year 2024/25 – General Income		
Rate	**Taxable Income**	
20%	(Basic rate)	up to £37,700
40%	(Higher rate)	£37,701 to £125,140
45%	(Additional rate)	over £125,140

Note that there are other tax rates for savings and investment income (interest and dividends) – we will look at these later in the book.

Note also that the above bands apply in the UK except Scotland. The calculation of Income Tax for residents in Scotland is not required in our studies.

This diagram shows how it works:

general taxable income

```
                               45% rate
£125,140  ----------------------------------------

                               40% rate
£37,700   ----------------------------------------

                               20% rate
£0        ----------------------------------------
```

So, for example, if an individual had taxable general income (after deducting their personal allowance) of £20,000 in 2024/25, the tax would be:

£20,000 × 20% = £4,000.00

Remember that 'income' can include not only earnings from a job but also other forms of income.

The total Income Tax relating to a tax year is often referred to as the 'Income Tax Liability'. We will now use a Case Study to show the full process for a simple tax computation.

Case Study

SHELLEY BEECH: BASIC INCOME TAX COMPUTATION

Shelley Beech works as an employee for a recruitment company. In 2024/25 she received £45,000 in income from this job, before her employer deducted £6,486 in Income Tax through PAYE.

She also received rent from the house that she had originally been left by her grandfather. The taxable amount of rent for 2024/25 has already been worked out as £15,500, but she hasn't paid any Income Tax on this yet.

Shelley is entitled to the personal allowance of £12,570 for the tax year.

required

Using an Income Tax computation, calculate the total Income Tax that Shelley is liable to pay for the tax year 2024/25, and how much of this amount has not yet been paid.

solution

Following the format discussed earlier, we can produce an Income Tax computation as follows:

Shelley Beech – Income Tax Computation for 2024/25

	£	£ Tax Paid
Employment Income	45,000	6,486
Property Income (rent)	15,500	–
Total Income	60,500	6,486
less Personal Allowance	12,570	
Taxable Income	47,930	

Income Tax Calculation

£37,700 × 20%		7,540.00
£10,230 × 40%		4,092.00
£47,930	Total Income Tax	11,632.00
	less already paid	6,486.00
	Income Tax to pay	5,146.00

To understand the above computation, you should note the following:

- The tax deducted at source is noted in the column on the right. The total of this column is then used in the final calculation to work out how much of the total tax is still unpaid.

- In this Case Study the taxable income of £47,930 is more than the £37,700 that forms the upper point of the 20% tax band. This means that the entire 20% band is used, as well as some of the 40% band. The income is not high enough to reach the 45% tax band.

- The amount of taxable income to be taxed at 40% is calculated by deducting the amounts charged at 20% from the taxable income (£47,930 – £37,700 = £10,230).

EXEMPT INCOME

Exempt income is outside the scope of Income Tax. Exempt income will not have had tax deducted from it at source, and it should not appear anywhere in the Income Tax computation. You should make sure that you are familiar with the following abbreviated list of exempt income, since it is possible that items from it could be included in an examination task to test your ability to select the right income to include in a tax computation.

- Prizes are generally exempt from Income Tax. These include:
  - Premium Bond prizes
  - Lottery prizes (of any amount)
  - betting winnings (unless a professional gambler)
- Income from ISAs is specifically exempt. This form of investment has been designed by the government to encourage saving and investment by exempting the income from tax.
- Household support fund payments are exempt from Income Tax. These are payments made by government to help with the cost of living.
- Damages arising from personal injury or death.
- Educational grants.

We will look at savings and investment income in detail in Chapter 3.

We will now use a further Case Study to see how some of the issues covered in this chapter can be dealt with all together.

Case Study

MARK DOWNE: INCOME FROM VARIOUS SOURCES

Mark Downe is a self-employed market trader. His profits (adjusted for Income Tax purposes) for the tax year were £40,000.

He also has income from a house that he rents out to students. The following profits from this have been calculated and adjusted for tax purposes.

6/4/2023 - 5/4/2024   £10,500

6/4/2024 - 5/4/2025   £13,000

Mark won £12,000 on the National Lottery on 15 June 2024.

He was also employed as a part-time barman from 1/7/2024 to 30/6/2025. He was paid on the last day of each month that he worked, and his monthly gross pay during this time was £500. He paid £900 under PAYE in 2024/25, and £300 in 2025/26.

Mark invested in an ISA in 2024/25. This generated interest of £120 in that tax year.

required

Using an Income Tax computation, calculate Mark's Income Tax liability for 2024/25.

solution

This is more complicated than the last Case Study, since we are given a lot more information about the taxpayer's income, some of which relates to a different tax year, and some of which is not taxable at all.

The income that should go into the tax computation for 2024/25 comprises:

- the profits from his self-employment of £40,000
- the rental income for the period 6/4/2024 to 5/4/2025: £13,000
- the part-time bar work earnings received in 2024/25, ie between 1/7/2024 and 5/4/2025, 9 months x £500 = £4,500

The lottery winnings and the interest from the ISA are both exempt.

We can now complete the Income Tax computation as follows:

Mark Downe – Income Tax Computation for 2024/25

	£	£ Tax Paid
Trading Income	40,000	–
Employment Income	4,500	900
Property Income (rent)	13,000	–
Total Income tax	57,500	900
less Personal Allowance	12,570	
Taxable Income	44,930	

Income Tax Calculation

£37,700 × 20%		7,540.00
£7,230 × 40%		2,892.00
£44,930	Income Tax Liability	10,432.00
	less already paid	900.00
	Income Tax to pay	9,532.00

RESPONSIBILITIES OF THE TAXPAYER

The taxpayer should always be open and honest in any dealings with HMRC. **It is the taxpayer's responsibility to inform HMRC if they have any taxable income or gains on which tax has not been paid.**

If the taxpayer normally receives a tax return or submits one online, then all taxable income and gains should be notified on the return. If the taxpayer does not normally need to complete a return, then it is the taxpayer's responsibility to inform HMRC of any source of income that HMRC is not aware of and they will then need to complete a tax return.

For those who do not normally complete a tax return, income that has tax deducted at source (for example employment income taxed under PAYE) does not need to be notified. However, where no tax has been deducted from income from some source(s) then it is the taxpayer's responsibility to notify HMRC. This could relate, for example, to rent received.

There is a general time limit for notifying HMRC about sources of taxable income (called 'notification of chargeability') which is 5 October following the end of the tax year. There are penalties for not complying with this.

tax planning, tax avoidance and tax evasion

Tax planning involves looking at an individual's or a company's financial planning from a tax perspective. The purpose of tax planning is to see how to accomplish all the other elements of the financial plan in the most tax-efficient manner, and so minimise tax. Tax planning should only involve legal and ethical methods of minimising the tax liability.

It is important to distinguish between the legal practice of tax avoidance, and tax evasion, which is illegal. Tax avoidance involves using legitimate tax rules and allowances to minimise the amount of tax that is due. This could include investing in ISAs so that any interest received is tax free.

Tax evasion involves using illegal methods to escape paying the correct amount of tax. Examples would include entering false information in a tax return or failing to notify HMRC about a taxable source of income on which tax has not been paid. Those who carry out tax evasion risk criminal prosecution.

While tax avoidance and tax evasion may appear to be easily distinguishable at each end of the scale, there will always be situations that may not be so clear cut. In particular, some 'tax avoidance schemes' have been developed that may not be legal.

HMRC has stated that where a scheme relies on **concealment, pretence, non-disclosure or misrepresentation** of the true facts then this is **illegal tax evasion.**

The government has developed various ways by which it hopes to prevent so-called 'aggressive' tax avoidance schemes. Tax avoidance schemes need to be disclosed to HMRC, who will then investigate the schemes to ensure that they are legal. HMRC has stated that using a tax avoidance scheme marks the individual out as a high-risk taxpayer, and that this will lead to close scrutiny of all their tax affairs, not just those involving the tax avoidance scheme.

In 2013 legislation was introduced to outlaw some schemes that were deemed to be 'abusive'. This legislation is known as the 'General Anti-Abuse Rule' (GAAR). It is based on the rejection of the old approach taken by the Courts that taxpayers are free to use their ingenuity to reduce their tax bills by any lawful means, however contrived those means might be.

In broad terms, the GAAR outlaws action taken by a taxpayer to achieve a favourable tax result that Parliament **did not anticipate** when it introduced the tax rules in question, where that course of action cannot **'reasonably be regarded as reasonable'.**

This 'double reasonableness test' sets a high threshold for HMRC to prove that an arrangement is abusive and therefore illegal.

Aggressive tax avoidance schemes are certainly unethical and rely on taxpayers not paying their fair share of tax.

The key to using legal tax avoidance measures is to only use tax rules in the way that they were originally intended by Parliament. So the use of ISAs to avoid paying tax on savings interest is entirely proper, since it is in line with the original intention of the legislation.

In general, anyone who suspects that tax evasion is being carried out is advised to report this to HMRC. This can be done anonymously. HMRC advises the person reporting not to attempt to discover any more information about the suspected tax evasion, and not to tell anyone else.

In the next section we will see how the AAT code of professional ethics deals with situations where a client is suspected of tax evasion. It is important that the code is followed in these circumstances.

THE DUTIES AND RESPONSIBILITIES OF A TAX PRACTITIONER

A **tax practitioner** is someone who helps clients on a professional basis with their tax affairs. The practitioner has responsibilities both:

- to the client, and
- to HM Revenue & Customs

The greatest duty of care is to the client, but the tax practitioner must always act within the law.

The AAT has published a revised 'Code of Professional Ethics' that deals with these and other issues. These apply to AAT students and members. The document can be downloaded from the website at www.aat.org.uk.

With regard to **confidentiality** in general, the guidelines state that confidentiality should always be observed unless either:

- authority has been given to disclose the information (by the client), or
- there is a legal or professional right or duty to disclose information

The Code also says that:

> 'Information about a past, present, or prospective client's or employer's affairs, or the affairs of clients of employers, acquired in a work context is likely to be confidential if it is not a matter of public knowledge.'

The rules of confidentiality apply in a social environment as well as a business one, and care should be taken to not inadvertently disclose confidential information. The need to comply also extends after a business relationship has ended – for example if there was a change of employment.

One important **exception to the normal rules of confidentiality** is where **'money laundering'** is known or suspected. 'Money laundering' includes any process of concealing or disguising the proceeds of any criminal offence, including tax evasion.

Where a practitioner has knowledge or suspicion that his client is money laundering, then he has a duty to inform the relevant person or authority. For those in a group practice this would be the Money Laundering Reporting Officer (MLRO), and for sole practitioners the National Crime Agency (NCA).

It is an offence to warn the client that a report of this type is going to be made about them. Money laundering therefore is not a situation where authority would be sought from the client to disclose information!

The Code states the following regarding taxation services:

'A member providing professional tax services has a duty to put forward the best position in favour of a client or an employer. However, the service must be carried out with professional competence, must not in any way impair integrity or objectivity, and must be consistent with the law.'

The Code also states that:

'A member shall only undertake taxation work on the basis of full disclosure by the client or employer. The member, in dealing with the tax authorities, must act in good faith and exercise care in relation to facts and information presented on behalf of the client or employer. It will normally be assumed that facts and information on which business tax computations are based were provided by the client or employer as the taxpayer, and the latter bears ultimate responsibility for the accuracy of the facts, information and tax computations. The member shall avoid assuming responsibility for the accuracy of facts, etc. outside his or her knowledge.

'When a member learns of a material error or omission in a tax return of a prior year, or of a failure to file a required tax return, the member has a responsibility to advise promptly the client or employer of the error or omission and recommend that disclosure be made to HMRC. If the client or employer, after having had a reasonable time to reflect, does not correct the error, the member shall inform the client or employer in writing that it is not possible for the member to act for them in connection with that return or other related information submitted to the authorities.'

Dealing with professional ethics can be a difficult and complex area, and we have only outlined some main points. If you find yourself in a position where you are uncertain how you should proceed because of an ethical problem then you should first approach your supervisor or manager. If you are still unable to resolve the problem then further professional or legal advice may need to be obtained.

The accountancy bodies (including the AAT) have published 'Professional Conduct in Relation to Taxation' (PCRT) documents.

The AAT reference material (which will be available as pop-ups in your assessment) is reproduced in the appendix to this book. This includes the information relating to the following PCRT help sheets:

- PCRT Help sheet A: Submission of tax information and 'Tax filings'
- PCRT Help sheet B: Tax advice
- PCRT Help sheet C: Dealing with errors
- PCRT Help sheet D: Requests for data by HMRC

You should study all the information provided in the reference material to ensure that you can apply it to situations that are presented to you in your assessment.

RESIDENCE AND DOMICILE

Individuals that are both **UK resident and UK domiciled** will be subject to UK tax on their **worldwide income and gains** – not just those arising in the UK. In order to gain some understanding of the complex rules regarding this area, we need to understand what is meant by residence and domicile.

residence

UK residence is determined by some specific tests that are applied to the individual for each tax year. The tests are based on facts about the time spent living and working in the UK. At one extreme, an individual who stays and works in the UK all year will clearly be a UK resident. At the other extreme, an individual who spends no time in the UK and who works abroad will not be a UK resident. The following tests are used to determine the residence status of individuals who fall between these two extremes.

The following tests need to be applied separately to each tax year to determine an individual's residence status. The tests fall into three groups. If a taxpayer satisfies an **'automatically resident'** test, then the individual will be a UK resident and no further tests are required. If the taxpayer satisfies an **'automatically not resident'** test, then they will not be a UK resident for that tax year without needing further tests. Where neither of these tests produces an outcome, then the **'resident by ties'** tests will be applied to determine the status.

These tests are complicated, but a summary is included in the AAT reference material, which will be available as pop-ups in your assessment, and is reproduced in the appendix to this book.

automatically resident test

- an individual will be a UK resident if they spend 183 days or more in the UK in the tax year, or
- an individual will be a UK resident if their only home was in the UK for at least 91 days in the tax year, and they spent at least 30 days in the tax year there.

automatically not resident tests

- an individual will **not** be a UK resident if they were a UK resident in at least one of the previous three tax years, and they spend fewer than 16 days in the tax year in the UK, or
- an individual will **not** be a UK resident if they were not a UK resident in any of the previous three tax years, and they spend fewer than 46 days in the tax year in the UK, or
- an individual will **not** be a UK resident if they work full-time overseas over the tax year, and they spend fewer than 91 days in the tax year in the UK, and work in the UK for fewer than 31 days.

resident by ties tests

The following tests are only used for individuals that are not either 'automatically resident' or 'automatically not resident' according to the above tests.

For individuals who were **UK resident** in at least **one** of the previous **three tax years**, the following five situations are considered as 'ties' and need to be taken into account in determining residence status:

- a family tie – has a spouse, civil partner, co-habitee or child under 18 years of age that is a UK resident
- an accommodation tie – has a place to live in the UK that is available for a continuous period of at least 91 days in the tax year
- a work tie – worked in the UK for at least 40 days in the tax year
- a 90 day tie – spent at least 90 days in the UK in either or both of the two tax years immediately preceding the year in question
- a country tie – was in the UK for more days than in any other individual country

The number of ties to the UK that an individual has is then considered along with the time spent in the UK to determine residence.

An individual will be a UK resident if they meet the criteria in the following table.

Days spent in UK during the tax year	Number of UK ties needed
16 - 45	At least 4
46 - 90	At least 3
91 - 120	At least 2
Over 120	At least 1

For individuals who were **not UK resident** in **any** of the previous **three tax years**, the above list of types of ties also applies, except the country tie. The following table shows the criteria to be a UK resident in these circumstances.

Days spent in UK during the tax year	Number of UK ties needed
46 - 90	At least 4
91 - 120	At least 3
Over 120	At least 2

worked examples

For the following individuals, work out whether they are UK residents for 2024/25, and which tests are used to determine this status.

Mr A has worked exclusively in the UK for several years. On 30 November 2024 he took a job in Sweden, and moved there, giving up his UK home.

Mr A will be a UK resident for 2024/25. He satisfies the automatic residence test, as he was in the UK for more than 183 days.

Miss B was a UK resident in 2022/23, but not in 2023/24. She worked full time in Australia throughout 2024/25, except for a 6-week holiday that she spent in the UK, during which she worked for five days.

Miss B will not be a UK resident. The 'automatically not resident' test applies to her, since she is working throughout the tax year in Australia, her time in the UK was fewer than 91 days, and her working time was fewer than 31 days.

Mrs C's job involves working in various countries, and she maintains a local home in each as necessary. She has a spouse who is a UK resident, and she shares a UK home with him when she is in the UK. The UK home is available to her all year. She has not been a UK resident for the last three years (nor spent more than 90 days in the UK in each of those years). In 2024/25 she worked in the UK from 1 August to 23 September (inclusive).

Neither of the automatic tests apply to Mrs C. She does not satisfy the automatic residency test, as she was in the UK for only 54 days (fewer than 183), and the UK home was not her only home. She does not satisfy the 'automatically not resident' test as she spent more than 46 days in the UK, and she did not work exclusively overseas.

Applying the ties test, Mrs C has three UK ties – her spouse is a UK resident, she has a UK home that is available to her for at least 91 days, and she has worked in the UK for over 40 days. By spending 54 days in the UK (between 46 and 90), she would need at least four UK ties to be considered a UK resident. She is therefore not a UK resident for 2024/25.

domicile

Domicile is broadly where an individual has a permanent home and where he or she intends to stay. Domicile of origin is based on the domicile of the individual's father or mother, and will become the individual's domicile unless positive action is taken to change it. This could be in the form of settling in a different country and making a will under the laws of that country. It is only possible to have one domicile country at any one time.

In April 2017 **deemed domicile** rules came into effect. This means that those people who meet either 'Condition A' or 'Condition B' will be treated for tax purposes as **UK domiciled**, and will be assessed to UK tax on worldwide income and gains on an arising basis.

Condition A applies to those who:

- were born in the UK, and
- have the UK as domicile of origin, and
- were resident in the UK for that tax year

Condition B applies to those who have been UK resident for at least 15 of the 20 tax years immediately before the relevant tax year.

Those to whom either of these conditions apply will not be able to claim the remittance basis (see below).

Where an individual is **UK resident**, but **not domiciled** (or deemed domiciled) in the UK, they will be taxed in full on any UK income and gains. Where they have income and gains that arise overseas, these non UK domiciled individuals (sometimes known as 'non-doms') will be taxed either:

- on an 'arising basis'. This means UK taxed on worldwide income and gains regardless of where they take place – just like a UK domiciled individual, or
- on a 'remittance basis'. This means that UK tax is only applied to the proceeds of any worldwide income and gains that are brought into the UK. To be taxed on a remittance basis the individual must pay a 'remittance basis charge' of either £30,000 or £60,000 for each tax year. Clearly it would only make sense to apply for the remittance basis if the individual had substantial overseas income or gains which were not going to be brought into the UK

The above is a brief summary of the very complex rules that apply in these situations.

When we examine Inheritance Tax in Chapter 7 we will also note the impact of domicile on that tax.

THYME TRAVELLER: RESIDENCE AND DOMICILE

situation

John Thyme was born in the UK, and he had the UK as his domicile of origin. In 2013 he moved to New Zealand to work. He made that country his domicile of choice.

In September 2023 his New Zealand employer offered him a two-year secondment to their UK offices, and he took up the offer and moved to the UK. He plans to return to New Zealand in September 2025, and continue to live there.

required

State, with reasons, how John will be treated for the tax year 2024/25 in terms of UK residence, domicile, and payment of UK tax.

solution

John will be considered a UK resident for 2024/25, since he satisfies the automatic residence test by being in the UK for more than 183 days in the tax year.

John will be considered as deemed UK domiciled, as he satisfies Condition A. He was born in the UK, has the UK as domicile of origin, and was UK resident for 2024/25.

Since he is deemed UK domiciled, John cannot claim the remittance basis for UK tax. He will be taxed on his worldwide income and gains on an arising basis for 2024/25.

Chapter Summary

- Tax systems have been developed based on various principles. These include equity, simplicity, convenience, stability, neutrality, efficiency and flexibility.

- Tax structures can be progressive, proportional or regressive. These terms refer to the proportion of income or wealth that is taken in tax.

- Income Tax in the UK is administered by HM Revenue & Customs. HMRC is responsible for publishing documents and forms to gather information about how much tax is owed, and collecting the tax on behalf of the government. It is governed by statute law and case law.

- Income is divided into categories so that appropriate rules can be applied to calculate the amount of each different form of income.

- Income Tax is calculated separately for each tax year, which runs from 6 April to the following 5 April. An Income Tax computation is used to calculate the tax by totalling the income from various sources, and subtracting allowances. The Income Tax is then calculated by reference to the tax bands and rates that relate to the tax year.

- Some specific forms of income are exempt from Income Tax and should not be included in the tax computation.

- It is the taxpayer's responsibility to inform HMRC if they have any taxable income or gains on which tax has not been paid. Taxpayers may use tax planning and ethical tax avoidance to minimise tax, but should not use aggressive tax avoidance schemes or tax evasion.

- The tax practitioner has duties of care to both the client and HMRC. The AAT Code of Professional Ethics deals with various situations relating to tax practitioners.

- Those who are UK resident and UK domiciled or deemed domiciled pay UK tax on their worldwide income and gains. UK residents who are not UK domiciled can elect to pay tax on their overseas income and gains on a remittance basis (ie only subject to UK tax if it is brought into the UK), but there is a substantial charge.

Key Terms

principles of taxation	the basic concepts that can guide those developing a tax system
principle of equity	the idea based on the fairness of a tax system
principle of simplicity	the concept that tax rules are transparent and understandable and certain
principle of convenience	the timing and method of tax collection should be as convenient as practical for taxpayers
principle of stability	taxes should be predictable, and not change too radically or frequently
principle of neutrality	the concept that taxes should not change behaviour – this does not have universal agreement
principle of efficiency	the costs involved in administering and collecting taxes should be minimised
principle of flexibility	tax systems should be able to keep pace with changes in technology and commerce
direct tax	a tax that is levied on the individual or organisation that generates the income or profits
indirect tax	a tax that is charged on goods or services
tax base	the total of the income or assets that a tax can be applied to
progressive tax	a tax which makes up a larger proportion of the income of those with higher incomes
proportional tax	a tax which makes up the same proportion of every individual's income
regressive tax	a tax which makes up a greater proportion of the income of those with lower incomes
statute law	legislation that is passed by parliament – an example of statute law relating to taxation is the Finance Act 2024
case law	the result of decisions taken in court cases that have an impact on the interpretation of law
tax year	each tax year runs from 6 April to the following 5 April – tax years are also known as fiscal years
basis of assessment	the rule that decides what income from a particular source is taxable for a tax year

introduction to taxation 27

Income Tax computation	the format used to calculate Income Tax – it collates income from various sources, subtracts personal allowances, and calculates tax on the resultant taxable income
personal allowance	the amount that an individual's income can amount to before tax is charged – in 2024/25 the personal allowance is £12,570
taxable income	an individual's income after subtracting the personal allowance – it is the amount that is used to calculate the tax liability
tax bands	Income Tax is charged at various percentage rates according to the type of income and the tax bands – for example the 20% tax band for general income in 2024/25 relates to taxable income up to £37,700
exempt income	income that is not chargeable to Income Tax and should therefore not be shown on the tax return or in the tax computation
tax planning	carrying out financial planning in the most tax-efficient way in order to minimise tax
tax avoidance	minimising tax by legal means (unless avoidance is 'abusive')
tax evasion	illegally relying on concealment, pretence, non-disclosure or misrepresentation to pay less tax
UK residence	an individual's residence for a tax year is based on rules concerning where the person lived and worked
automatically resident tests	tests which can determine if an individual is UK resident for a certain tax year, without further requirements
automatically not resident tests	tests which can determine if an individual is not a UK resident in a certain tax year, without further requirements
resident by ties tests	tests that are used if the automatic tests are inconclusive – these tests rely on ties to the UK in combination with days spent in the UK within the tax year
domicile	a person's domicile is the country that they intend to live in permanently
arising basis	the tax basis that applies to worldwide income and gains as they arise
remittance basis	the tax basis that only applies to the amount of overseas income or gains that is brought into the UK

Activities

Note: in these Student Activities the words 'year end' are abbreviated to 'y/e' and dates are quoted in the format '30/9/09'.

1.1 Analyse the following list of statements by ticking the appropriate column.

		True	False
(a)	All tax systems are based on exactly the same set of principles, which are enshrined in international law and cannot be deviated from		
(b)	The principle of equity is concerned with fairness		
(c)	Vertical equity means that all taxpayers should pay the same amount of tax		
(d)	Neutrality is a concept that not all tax systems adhere to since tax can be used to try to change behaviour		
(e)	A progressive tax system is one in which the proportion of income paid in tax rises for higher income levels		
(f)	A tax system that charges every taxpayer the same amount of money is a proportional system		

introduction to taxation

1.2 The following are statements made by a trainee in the tax department. Select those statements that are true.

		True	False
(a)	One of the reasons that income is divided into categories is so that the correct rules can be applied to each type of income		
(b)	When examining the tax rules for 2024/25, the only law that is relevant is the Finance Act 2024		
(c)	Every individual will receive a tax return each year that they must complete		
(d)	All income must be declared on the tax return and used in the Income Tax computation		
(e)	Taxable income is the name given to total income (apart from exempt income) after the personal allowance has been subtracted		
(f)	An individual with only general taxable income of £1,500 in 2024/25 would pay Income Tax of £300		
(g)	It is the job of a tax practitioner to ensure that his client pays the least amount of tax. This may involve bending the rules, or omitting certain items from a tax computation		
(h)	Most self-employed people pay tax under PAYE and so don't have to worry about completing tax returns		
(i)	A lottery win of over £250,000 is taxable		

1.3 Mary has the following income:

Salary of £1,000 per month from her employment throughout 2024 and 2025, plus bonuses paid as follows:

£300 paid in May 2024 re y/e 31/12/23

£500 paid in May 2025 re y/e 31/12/24

Mary had nothing deducted under PAYE during 2024/25.

Part-time self-employed business – adjusted profits as follows:

y/e 5/4/25 £2,800

She also rents out a property that she owns. She received £4,500 in rent for the period 6/4/24 - 5/4/25 after deducting allowable costs.

Required:

Using an Income Tax Computation for 2024/25, calculate Mary's total Income Tax liability, and how much of it has not been paid.

1.4 The following is a list of the sources of Sue's income for the tax year.

(a) Dividends from shares in UK companies
(b) Income from employment as a Sales Manager
(c) Interest from an ISA
(d) Interest from a bank deposit account
(e) Winnings from a bet on the Grand National
(f) Rent received from a property let to students

Required:

For each income source either state which category it should be included under, or state that it is exempt from Income Tax.

1.5 John has the following income:
- wages from employment £900 per month
- rental income from a house left to him by his Grandmother, due on the last day of each month. The £500 per month for the months of April 2024 - March 2025 were paid on time
- there were no allowable expenses to be deducted from this rental income (ignore any Property Allowance)
- interest Earned on ISA with B&B Building Society, £230

John paid nothing during 2024/25 under PAYE.

Required:

Using an Income Tax Computation for the tax year, calculate John's total Income Tax liability, and how much of it has not been paid.

1.6 Megan has the following income:

Salary of £2,800 per month from her employment throughout 2024 and 2025, plus bonuses paid as follows:

£800 paid in September 2024 re y/e 31/3/24

£500 paid in September 2025 re y/e 31/3/25

Megan had £4,366 deducted under PAYE during 2024/25.

Income from writing articles for technical magazines, categorised as trading income, as follows:

year ended 5/4/25   £24,700

Required:

Using an Income Tax Computation for the tax year, calculate Megan's total Income Tax liability, and how much of it has not been paid.

1.7 Analyse the following list of statements by ticking the appropriate column.

		True	False
(a)	It is the taxpayer's responsibility to inform HMRC if they have any taxable income on which tax has not been paid		
(b)	If tax evasion is suspected then HMRC should generally be informed. If the suspected tax evader is a client then the AAT Code of Professional Ethics should also be followed		
(c)	Clients should not be advised to invest in ISAs in case they are considered to be evading tax		
(d)	A tax scheme that relies on concealment, pretence, non-disclosure or misrepresentation of the true facts is illegal tax evasion		
(e)	All UK taxpayers can choose to pay tax based on the remittance basis		
(f)	Taxpayers who are UK resident and UK domiciled only incur UK tax on income and gains that originate in the UK		

1.8 Chloe has worked full time in Singapore since 2022. During 2024/25 she was asked by her employer to work at their UK office for 28 days. She agreed to do this and arranged to take a 30-day holiday in the UK immediately after her work in the UK. She then returned to Singapore.

Work out whether Chloe is a UK resident for 2024/25, and explain which tests are used to determine this status.

1.9 Bernard was a UK resident in 2022/23, but not in 2023/24. He lived and worked in the UK for 60 days during 2024/25. He has two ties to the UK.

Explain whether Bernard is a UK resident for 2024/25.

2 Income from property

this chapter covers...

In this chapter we will examine how income from rented UK property is taxed. We will start by examining what exactly is covered by the rules that we need to learn, and then see how the 'cash' basis or 'accruals' basis is applied to this type of income.

We will look in detail at the expenditure that is 'allowable' – that which can reduce the taxable amount. We will contrast this with disallowable expenditure, and see how a calculation of taxable profit is carried out for both individual and multiple properties.

HOW PROPERTY INCOME IS TAXED

what does Property Income cover?

Property income can include:

- income from renting out land
- income from renting out unfurnished property
- income from renting out furnished property

The term 'property' is used to mean buildings, either residential (flats, houses, etc) or commercial (offices etc).

You may be asked to calculate the amount assessable relating to one or more properties that are rented out by a client. The client is usually the owner of the properties, but it would be possible for him to have rented them from another landlord. The landlord may have bought the property specifically to rent out. This is known as 'buy to let'.

basis of calculation

The basis of calculation of property income is normally the amount **received** during the tax year less the amount **paid** during the tax year for allowable expenses. This 'cash basis' is a recent change from the previous accruals basis, and the cash basis applies to individuals with annual property receipts of up to £150,000. Those with gross rental income over £150,000 will automatically be taxed on an accruals basis. Individuals below the £150,000 level may elect to use the accruals basis if they wish, but throughout this book we will normally assume that the cash basis is used. You should assume that the cash basis is applicable in your examination, unless told otherwise.

As the **cash basis** only assesses income in the tax year that it is received, the issue of dealing with irrecoverable rent does not arise. Irrecoverable rent will not have been received, so will not be assessed. The point at which rent is due is not relevant in our calculations when using the cash basis.

If the **accruals basis** is to be used (either because the taxpayer has opted to do so, or because the annual gross rental income exceeds £150,000), then the property income calculation must be based on income and expenditure relating to the tax year. This is irrespective of when the cash is received or paid.

When the accruals basis is used, one issue to be careful about is where an unpaid amount of rent is considered 'irrecoverable'. In these circumstances the irrecoverable amount can be deducted from the rental income. This is exactly the same logic that occurs in financial accounting, when 'irrecoverable debts' are written off.

Case Study

MINNIE STREET: ASSESSABLE RENT

Minnie Street rents out two unfurnished properties to tenants. Each has a monthly rental of £500, payable in advance on the 6th day of each month.

From January 2024 onwards, the following rents were paid:

The tenant of property one paid the rent on time every month during 2024. On 6 January 2025 he paid six months' rent in advance since he was going on a long holiday.

The tenant of property two also paid the rent on time every month during 2024. During 2025 he failed to pay any rent. He left the property on 5 March, without leaving a forwarding address or paying the rent that he owed. Minnie has been unable to locate him since then. Property two was re-let to another tenant in May 2025.

The only allowable expenditure relating to the properties was buildings insurance. This was as follows:

The insurance for the calendar year 2024 was £360 per property. This was paid in December 2023.

The insurance for the calendar year 2025 was £480 per property. This was paid in December 2024.

required

Calculate the assessable property income for 2024/25 for each of the two properties, assuming that

(1) The cash basis is used, and

(2) Minnie opts to use the accruals basis.

Ignore the property allowance (see later in chapter).

solution

(1) Cash Basis

	Property One £	Property Two £
Rent received	7,500	4,500
less insurance paid	(480)	(480)
Assessable property income	7,020	4,020

Using the cash basis we are concerned with amounts received or paid during the tax year, regardless of the period that they relate to.

(2) Accruals Basis

	Property One £	Property Two £
Rent receivable	6,000	5,500
less		
Irrecoverable rent (Jan & Feb)		(1,000)
Insurance relating to 2024/25	(390)	(390)
Assessable property income	5,610	4,110

Using the accruals basis we incorporate the income and expenditure that relates to the tax year 2024/25. The income is therefore twelve months' rent for property one, and eleven months' rent for property two. The insurance costs are made up of (9/12 x £360) + (3/12 x £480) = £390.

EXPENDITURE THAT IS ALLOWABLE

'Allowable' expenditure is expenditure that can be deducted from the rental income to arrive at the assessable property income.

Note that some expenditure that is quite proper from an accounting point of view may not be 'allowable' for taxation purposes. This does not mean that the accounts produced are necessarily wrong, but we will need to make adjustments before they are suitable for our tax work.

The general rule for expenditure to be allowable in a property income calculation is that it must be:

- revenue rather than capital in nature (except some replacement items – see later), and
- 'wholly and exclusively' for the purpose of lettings

Allowable expenditure may include:

- business rates, water rates and council tax – this would apply where the landlord has paid these items, effectively on behalf of the tenant; the rent would have been set at such a level to allow for the fact that the landlord was paying this cost
- rent paid to a 'superior' landlord – this would apply only if the property did not belong to the client, but was rented from someone else; the situation would therefore be one of 'subletting'
- insurance and management expenses
- costs of advertising for tenants
- ongoing repairs, maintenance and redecoration costs (but not those of a **capital** nature – see later)

- Flat rate mileage allowance for journeys undertaken in connection with the rental of properties, at the rates shown below

Vehicle type	First 10,000 business miles in tax year	Additional mileage
Cars and goods vehicles	45p per mile	25p per mile
Motorcycles	24p per mile	24p per mile

Expenditure that satisfies the above rules and is incurred before the premises are rented out or in periods in-between rental periods ('void' periods) is also generally allowable. However, such expenditure is not allowed during periods when the property is used privately – for example when a family member is living there without paying rent.

allowance for replacement items

Allowable expenditure also includes the replacement of domestic items such as furniture, furnishings, appliances (including 'white goods') and kitchenware. This only covers the replacement of items that existed in the property previously – it does not cover the expenditure on the first time that an item is purchased by the landlord. This is an important exception to the general rule that capital expenditure is not allowable.

So, for example, if a landlord rented out a property that included a cooker, the original cost of the cooker would not be allowable. If the cooker subsequently stopped working, a replacement cooker (of an equivalent type) would be an allowable cost.

Where there are disposal costs for the old item, these are also allowable, but where the old item is sold then the proceeds are deducted from the cost of the replacement.

The cost of replacements is allowable for both furnished and unfurnished property, and applies to both the cash basis and the accruals basis.

property allowance

As an **alternative** to deducting allowable expenditure, an individual may deduct up to £1,000 (per year) 'property allowance' from the total gross rental income of all properties. If the total gross rental income is £1,000 or less, this means that the property allowance will reduce the assessable amount to zero.

The application of the property allowance is automatic when gross income is up to £1,000 (but the taxpayer can elect not to use the property allowance). When the gross income is over £1,000, the taxpayer can elect to apply the property allowance if required. Any election relating to the property allowance must be made by 31 January, two years after the end of the tax year (ie one year after the latest date for submission of a tax return).

The logical approach is as follows:

- Where the allowable expenditure (calculated in the usual way) totals less than £1,000 (or is zero) then the property allowance of £1,000 should normally be claimed instead of the usual allowable expenditure. An exception is where the allowable expenditure exceeds the income, in which case a loss can be generated by claiming the normal allowable expenditure. A loss cannot be claimed by using the property allowance

- Where the allowable expenditure (calculated in the usual way) totals more than £1,000, then the property allowance should be ignored, and the allowable expenditure claimed as usual. This can apply even if the gross rental income is less than £1,000, since this will generate a loss which can be offset later

Note that the property allowance can only be claimed when no other allowable expenditure is deducted.

EXPENDITURE THAT IS NOT ALLOWABLE

Since only revenue expenditure (and some replacement expenditure) is allowable, it follows that most capital expenditure will not be allowable. Non-allowable capital expenditure includes the following:

- the **cost of the property itself** together with any initial purchase of furniture etc. Also considered as capital will be the costs connected with the purchase, including the legal and professional fees and Stamp Duty Land Tax incurred in buying the property

- the **cost of improvements.** This will apply when expenditure is incurred in upgrading or extending the property. For example, building a garage is an improvement, as is the installation of central heating where none existed previously. Note that normal ongoing repairs and maintenance when the property is simply brought back to its previous condition are allowable

- the **cost of renovations** carried out before a property is rented out for the first time. One argument for viewing this expenditure as capital is that the need for the renovations will have been reflected in the lower purchase price of the property

Other costs that are not allowable include the following:

- depreciation of any kind relating to capital expenditure
- expenditure not connected with the business of lettings (for example, expenditure on a private part of the property)

CALCULATING THE PROFIT OR LOSS UNDER PROPERTY INCOME

To arrive at the profit or loss under property income we need to:

- determine the assessable rents received, and
- deduct any allowable expenditure

The calculation of the profit or loss is known as a **property income computation.**

dealing with a single property

We will now present a Case Study involving a single property to show how this calculation can be carried out. We will use the information regarding allowable expenditure to help us (see pages 35 and 36).

Case Study

UNA LODGE: CALCULATING ASSESSABLE PROPERTY INCOME

Una Lodge rents out one furnished property. The following is a statement compiled from her accounting records relating to the period 6/4/2024 - 5/4/2025.

	£	£
Rental Income Received		12,000
less expenditure:		
Council Tax	800	
Water Rates	400	
Insurance	300	
Installing Central Heating	2,000	
Depreciation of Furniture	900	
Managing Agent's Charges	600	
Replacement of carpet	800	
		5,800
Profit		6,200

required

Calculate the assessable property income for Una Lodge.

solution

We can re-draft the profit statement, incorporating only allowable expenditure and deductions as follows:

Property Income Computation

	£	£
Rental Income		12,000
less allowable expenditure:		
Council Tax	800	
Water Rates	400	
Insurance	300	
Managing Agent's Charges	600	
Replacement of carpet	800	
		2,900
Assessable		9,100

Notes

- The installation of central heating is capital expenditure, and therefore not allowable for tax purposes.
- Depreciation is never allowable.
- The replacement of the carpet is allowable.

several properties

When there is more than one property, the best approach is to draw up a statement with one column for each property. The addition of a total column provides a means of double-checking your arithmetic, and sets out the figures needed for the tax return. Each property can then be dealt with in turn, and the overall result incorporated into one property income assessment figure. If one property then incurs a loss after adjustment for tax purposes, it should be offset against the assessable profits from the other properties. Using a columnar format like this enables the net result to be calculated quite easily, as in the Case Study which follows.

In a later section we will go on to see how to deal with a situation where the net effect of all the properties is a loss.

Case Study

ANDY LORD: PROFITS FROM SEVERAL PROPERTIES

Andy Lord rents out three properties in High Street. Property number one is unfurnished, while properties two and three are furnished.

Andy has provided the following statement relating to the properties for the period 6/4/2024 – 5/4/2025.

	Property 1		Property 2		Property 3	
	£	£	£	£	£	£
Rental Income		5,000		3,500		4,300
Less expenses:						
Council Tax	500		–		400	
Rent Payable	–		–		2,500	
Property Insurance	200		200		200	
Roof Repairs	1,300		–		–	
Other Repairs	6,500		2,490		200	
Replacement furniture	–		–		750	
Professional Fees for Debt Recovery	150		–		–	
Depreciation	500		500		500	
		9,150		3,190		4,550
Profit / (Loss)		(4,150)		310		(250)

You have also determined the following facts:

- property number two was occupied rent-free by Andy's student son until 5 September, when it was let out commercially to a tenant. The repairs were completed in December. The other expenses relate to the whole tax year
- the rent payable relates to property number three that is not owned by Andy Lord
- 'Roof Repairs' relates to the cost of repairing damage that occurred during a storm. This amount was not covered by the insurance policy
- 'Other Repairs' includes £2,900 paid to build a porch on property number one

required

Calculate the amount of assessable property income.

solution

	Property 1	Property 2	Property 3	Total
	£	£	£	£
Rental Income	5,000	3,500	4,300	12,800
Less allowable expenses:				
Council Tax	500	–	400	900
Rent Payable	–	–	2,500	2,500
Property Insurance	200	117	200	517
Roof Repairs	1,300	–	–	1,300
Other Repairs	3,600	2,490	200	6,290
Replacement furniture	–	–	750	750
Professional Fees for Debt Recovery	150	–	–	150
Assessable amount	(750)	893	250	393

Notes

- Property number two is only rented out commercially for seven months of the tax year. Therefore 7/12 of the property insurance expenses are allowable.
- The professional fees for debt recovery are wholly and exclusively for the rental business and therefore allowable.
- The roof repairs are allowable as revenue expenditure.
- The 'other repairs' are allowable, with the exception of the porch that is considered an improvement and therefore capital in nature.
- Depreciation is not allowable.
- The replacement furniture is allowable.
- The loss for property number one is offset against the profits on the other properties to give a 'property income' figure of £393.

DEALING WITH PROPERTY LOSSES

Earlier in this chapter we saw how a loss when renting one property is offset against profits for other properties in the same tax year.

However, if *either:*

- there are no other properties with profits in that tax year, or
- the net result from all the properties is a loss

then the following occurs:

- the property income assessment for the tax year is nil, and
- the loss must be carried forward until there is sufficient future property income to offset it

The property loss can only be set against future property income. If there are insufficient property income profits in the tax year that follows the loss, then the balance of the loss is carried forward again until it can be relieved.

Relief for losses is only available if the loss arises from commercial letting – not for property let to a friend or relative at a reduced rate.

The Case Study below demonstrates how property losses are relieved.

IVOR COST: DEALING WITH LOSSES

Ivor Cost rents out several properties. After amalgamating the rents from all his properties, and deducting all allowable expenses, he has arrived at the following figures:

Tax Year	Profit / (Loss)
	£
2022/23	(5,500)
2023/24	3,800
2024/25	6,400

required

Calculate the assessable property income for each of the three tax years referred to.

solution

Tax Year	Working	Property Income Assessment
2022/23	loss of £5,500 carried forward to next year	Nil
2023/24	£3,800 of loss used against profit of £3,800	Nil
	Balance of loss carried forward	
2024/25	Profit £6,400 less balance of loss £1,700	£4,700

income from property

Chapter Summary

- Income from renting land and property is assessed under 'property income'. The normal basis of assessment for this is the income received in the tax year, less allowable expenses, calculated on a cash basis. The calculation of the assessable amount is known as a property income computation.

- Allowable expenses are those wholly and exclusively for the business of lettings. Replacement of furniture and appliances is an allowable expense.

- Expenditure that is not allowable includes most capital expenditure and any form of depreciation.

- The property allowance of up to £1,000 can be claimed instead of normal allowable expenses.

- Where more than one property is let, the results are combined and any individual losses netted off against other properties with profits. Where the overall result is a loss, this is carried forward against future property income profits.

Key Terms

property income — the term used to categorise income from land and property (typically rental income)

cash basis — the basis where allowable cash payments are deducted from amounts received to arrive at the assessable amount

allowable expenditure — expenditure that may be deducted from receipts in the calculation of profits or losses for tax purposes

Activities

2.1 Julie rented out her unfurnished property from 6/7/2024, and received £5,000 for 12 months' rent in advance on that day. She also set up a direct debit payment of £25 per month for property insurance. In December 2024 she spent £200 replacing a broken fridge.

Calculate the assessable property income for 2024/25. Ignore the property allowance.

2.2 Dave bought an unfurnished flat on 6/11/2024, and immediately let it to a tenant for £400 per month, payable monthly. Dave paid £2,000 legal fees to acquire the flat. He paid £30 per month property insurance.

Dave used the services of an agent to collect the rent and liaise with the tenant. The agent charged £100 per month for this service, and deducted the fee from the rent paid over.

Calculate the assessable property income for 2024/25. Ignore the property allowance.

2.3 Anna Partement rents out one furnished property. The following is a statement compiled from her accounting records relating to the tax year:

	£	£
Rental Income Received		10,000
less expenditure:		
Council Tax	700	
Water Rates	300	
Insurance	400	
Cost of Replacement Carpets	2,500	
Depreciation of Furniture	800	
Managing Agent's Charges	1,000	
		5,700
Profit		4,300

Required:

Calculate the property income for Anna for the tax year.

2.4

Sonny Hill rents out three country cottages. All properties are furnished.

He has provided the following statement relating to the properties for the tax year:

	Property 1		Property 2		Property 3	
	£	£	£	£	£	£
Rental Income		8,000		6,000		5,500
Less expenses:						
Council Tax	800		650		400	
Managing Agent's Charges	1,600		1,200		1,100	
Property Insurance	400		300		250	
Redecoration	–		600		–	
Repainting Windows	500		450		500	
Other Repairs	2,900		400		200	
Accountancy Fees	150		150		150	
Purchase of furniture					2,800	
Depreciation	500		500		500	
		6,850		4,250		5,900
Profit / (Loss)		1,150		1,750		(400)

You have also determined the following facts:

- property number three was purchased on 6 June. This property was rented out from 6 July. The council tax on this property relates to the nine month period from 6 July. Other expenses relate to the ten month period from 6 June

- 'Other Repairs' includes £2,600 paid to install central heating in property number one where none had previously existed

- Sonny Hill has an unrelieved property income loss of £1,000 brought forward from the previous tax year

- the purchase of furniture for property three was made on 1 July

Required:

Calculate the property income for the tax year.

2.5 Maisey Nett rents out one furnished property. The following is a statement compiled from her accounting records relating to the tax year:

	£	£
Rental Income Received		11,500
less expenditure:		
Accountancy Fees	400	
Council Tax	650	
Water Rates	350	
Insurance	300	
Cost of Replacement Carpets	2,000	
Managing Agent's Charges	1,000	
	4,700	
Profit		6,800

Maisey also had gross income of £49,500 in the tax year from her job as a legal executive. She paid £7,386 Income Tax under PAYE.

Required:

(1) Calculate the property income for Maisey.

(2) Calculate Maisey's total Income Tax liability for the tax year, and the part of that amount that she has yet to pay.

2.6 Simon has two properties in addition to his home, details of which are as follows:

Three bedroom house:

(1) This unfurnished house is rented out for £900 per month. The property was occupied this tax year until 6 September when the tenants suddenly moved out, owing the rent for July and August. Simon knows that he will not recover this rent. The property was let again from 6 December to another family.

(2) The only expense paid by Simon on the house was 8% management charge to the agent on rent received.

One bedroom flat:

(3) This furnished flat is rented out for £450 per month. The property was unoccupied this tax year until 6 June when a couple moved in on a twelve month lease.

(4) Simon paid council tax and water rates on the flat, totalling £1,400 for the period in the tax year that the flat was occupied. He also paid insurance of £270 for the tax year.

Calculate the profit or loss made on each property, using the following table.

	Three bedroom house £	**One bedroom flat** £
Income		
Expenses:		

2.7 For the following alternative situations, select whether it would be more beneficial for the landlord to set the actual allowable costs against the gross property income, or to utilise the property allowance.

Situation	Use actual costs	Use property allowance
(a) Gross property income £4,500, Actual allowable costs £1,100		
(b) Gross property income £1,500, Actual allowable costs £900		
(c) Gross property income £500, Actual allowable costs £100		
(d) Gross property income £500, Actual allowable costs £900		

3 Income from savings and investments

this chapter covers...

In this chapter we examine the way that savings and investment income is taxed. This includes interest from banks and building societies and dividends from shares in UK companies.

We will learn that assessment is based on the amount received (not the accruals basis), and that income is received without deduction of tax at source.

We will then go on to see how dividend income has tax rates that are different to the rates for general and savings income. There is also a Personal Savings Allowance, and a Dividend Allowance that can usually reduce the tax within the bands.

Finally we summarise the sources of tax-free investment income.

THE BASIS OF ASSESSMENT FOR SAVINGS AND INVESTMENT INCOME

In this chapter we will examine savings and investment income and see how it is taxed. There are two types of savings and investment income. They are:

- interest received from various sources – typically banks and building societies
- dividends from shares held in limited companies

The basis of assessment for both interest and UK dividends is the gross amount **received in the tax year**. The period that the interest is based on is therefore irrelevant. Amounts received include money credited to an individual's bank or building society accounts during the tax year. In most situations there are no allowable expenses that can be deducted in the calculation of savings and investment income. The interest that we will be examining typically comes from banks and building societies, but can also arise from government securities (gilts) and various loans to organisations.

receiving income gross

The vast majority of interest (including all interest from banks and building societies) and all dividends is received gross – with no deduction of tax at source. This is part of a radical change made a few years ago in the taxation of interest and dividends which also includes a 'personal savings allowance' and a 'dividends allowance'. We will see shortly how these allowances work to reduce the tax on most individuals' savings and investment income.

TAX BANDS AND RATES FOR SAVINGS AND DIVIDEND INCOME

Although the tax rates for general income are 20%, 40% and 45% (as we saw in the last chapters), the rates for savings and dividend income are not always the same as these. Instead, savings income and dividend income each have their own tax rates that apply in the various tax bands.

Income from savings and dividends are the only exceptions to the general Income Tax rates that we saw in Chapter 1. We therefore have a total of three categories of income that have different tax rates:

- general income
- savings income, and
- dividend income

General income is any income except that from savings or dividends.

The following chart (which is not to scale) shows the tax bands and rates for these three types of income after deductions of the personal allowance, and is based on the tax year 2024/25.

	Tax bands and tax rates, 2024/25			
Additional Rate	45%	45%	39.35%	Dividend Additional Rate
£125,140				
Higher Rate	40%	40%	33.75%	Dividend Upper Rate
£37,700				
Basic Rate	20%	20%	8.75%	Dividend Ordinary Rate
£5,000				
Starting Rate		0%		
£0				
	General Income	Savings Income	Dividend Income	

Notice that the tax rates for dividends have slightly different names.

You can see from the chart that there is a special 0% starting rate that applies to savings income in certain circumstances, even though there is no equivalent starting rate for general income or dividend income. This starting rate only applies in the rare situations when the individual's taxable general income is below £5,000. These situations will not form part of your examination, and so will not be covered in this book. We have included the starting rate in the above chart for completeness, but we will omit it in future charts as it will not be examinable.

The 'personal savings allowance' and the 'dividends allowance' both operate within the other bands to provide further opportunities for tax-free investment income.

personal savings allowance

The personal savings allowance is in addition to, and separate from, the starting rate for savings income. It means that taxpayers with savings income that falls outside of the starting rate will pay 0% tax on savings income up to the following amounts:

- for basic rate taxpayers on savings income up to £1,000
- for higher rate taxpayers on savings income up to £500
- for additional rate taxpayers there is no tax-free amount

These allowances effectively sit inside the bands that would otherwise apply to the savings income and reduce the tax rate within the allowance to zero.

Where the savings income is greater than the allowance then the normal savings rates apply to the excess. The personal savings allowance cannot be greater than the individual's savings income, and cannot be used against general income or dividends.

Although this process is straightforward for those with not much savings income, it can become a little more complicated for others. In the Case Study that follows shortly we will illustrate exactly how it works.

dividend allowance

The dividend allowance applies to dividend income and works in a similar way to the personal savings allowance, but with only one universal amount. The tax-free allowance of up to £500 applies to individuals, regardless of which tax band they are in. If there is dividend income in excess of this then it is taxed at the applicable dividend rates. The dividend allowance cannot be greater than the individual's dividend income, and cannot be used against any other type of income.

using the rates and bands

It is vital when working out an individual's tax that the taxable income is analysed into these three categories, and that this analysis is clearly shown in your answers to exam questions. A specific order is followed when calculating tax on each category of income. This order is:

- general income; then
- savings income; and finally
- dividend income

Dividend income is therefore considered the 'top slice' of an individual's taxable income, with savings income the middle slice.

We will now use a series of examples to illustrate how the personal savings allowance and the dividend allowance work and fit into the tax bands.

---

example 1

Firstly, suppose an individual has the following taxable income, after setting off the personal allowance of £12,570.

- General income   £22,000
- Savings income   £750
- Dividend income   £400

We can see that the total taxable income is well below £37,700, so the individual will not be a higher rate taxpayer. The personal savings allowance will therefore be up to £1,000. The dividend allowance will be up to £500.

The tax calculation will look like this, going through the income types in order:

General income	£22,000 × 20% (all at the basic rate)	£4,400.00
Savings income	£750 × 0% (personal savings allowance)	£0.00
Dividend income	£400 × 0% (dividend allowance)	£0.00
Total tax liability		£4,400.00

Notice that the personal savings allowance and the dividend allowance are both restricted to the totals of the relevant type of income, and cannot reduce the tax on general income.

Now we will look at a more complex example. The taxpayer is also a basic rate taxpayer.

example 2

Suppose an individual has the following taxable income, after setting off the personal allowance of £12,570.

- General income   £14,300
- Savings income   £3,600
- Dividend income   £1,400

We can see that this individual will not be a higher rate taxpayer, and so will be entitled to a personal savings allowance of up to £1,000.

We will work up through the types of income, working out the tax as we go.

General income	£14,300	x 20% (all at the basic rate)	£2,860.00
Savings income	£1,000	x 0% (personal savings allowance)	£0.00
	£2,600	x 20% (the rest of the £3,600)	£520.00
Dividend income	£500	x 0% (dividend allowance)	£0.00
	£900	x 8.75% (the rest of the £1,400)	£78.75
Total tax liability			£3,458.75

The following diagram (which is not to scale) illustrates the process.

income from savings and investments

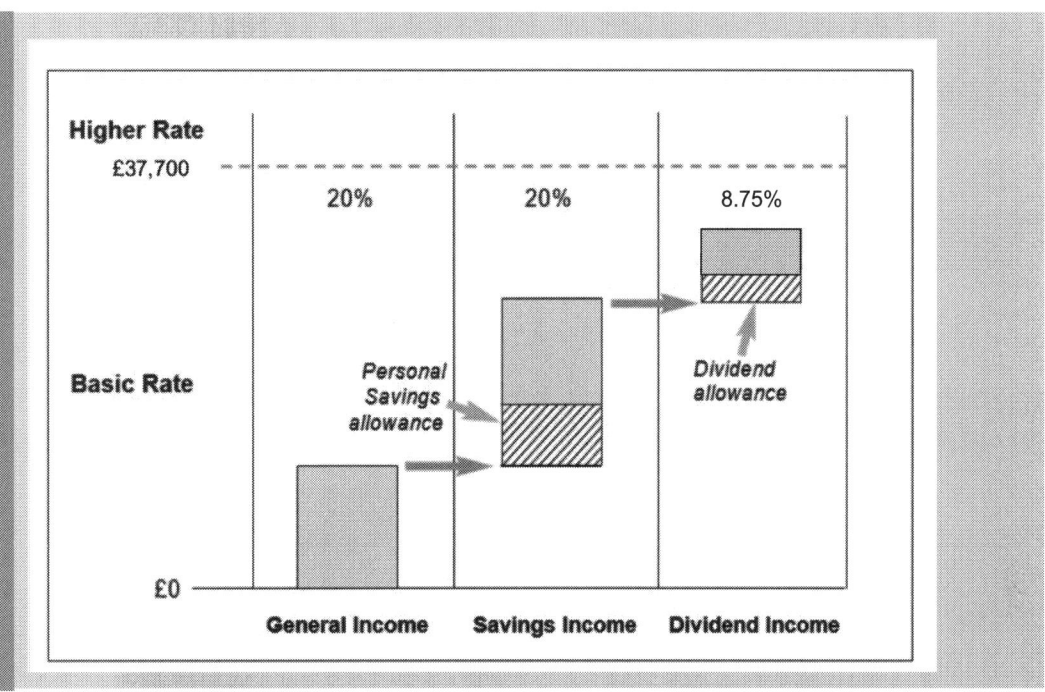

This third example is a little more complex, and involves the use of the higher rate as well as the basic rate bands.

example 3

Suppose someone has £72,500 taxable income (after deducting the personal allowance of £12,570), made up as follows for 2024/25:

- General income   £28,000
- Savings income   £12,000
- Dividend income   £32,500

The bands would be worked through, incorporating the personal savings allowance and dividend allowance as we progress.

We can see immediately that this individual is a higher rate taxpayer since the taxable income is well above £37,700, but not as high as £125,140. The personal savings allowance will therefore be £500 and the dividend allowance will be £500. Since the savings and dividends received are above these figures, tax will become due on the excess income.

The band levels apply to the whole income (including that covered by the personal savings allowance and dividend allowance), so that each time we move into the next type of income we use the cumulative income to determine the rate.

In our example this will work as follows:

General income	£28,000	x 20% (all at the basic rate)	£5,600.00
Savings income	£500	x 0% (personal savings allowance)	£0.00
	£9,200	x 20% (up to cumulative £37,700)	£1,840.00
	£2,300	x 40% (the rest of the savings income)	£920.00
	£12,000		
Dividend income	£500	x 0% (dividend allowance)	£0.00
	£32,000	x 33.75% (the rest of the dividends)	£10,800.00
	£32,500		
Total tax liability			£19,160.00

Notice that in this example part of the savings income is taxed at the higher rate, and the excess dividend income over the dividend allowance is taxed at the dividend upper rate.

The diagram on the next page (which is not to scale) illustrates how the system works, using the figures for the third example shown above. We have ignored the Additional Rate band in this diagram as the income is not high enough to use it. Notice how the bar representing each type of income starts at the level that the previous one ended. This is the key to understanding the system.

The personal allowance is normally deducted from the general income when analysing the taxable income. If there is insufficient general income to do this then the savings income is used, and finally dividend income.

To summarise:

- always work up the bands, following the order:
  - general income
  - savings income
  - dividend income
- incorporate the personal savings allowance and the dividend allowance in the bands
- always use the cumulative taxable income totals to determine the bands

income from savings and investments

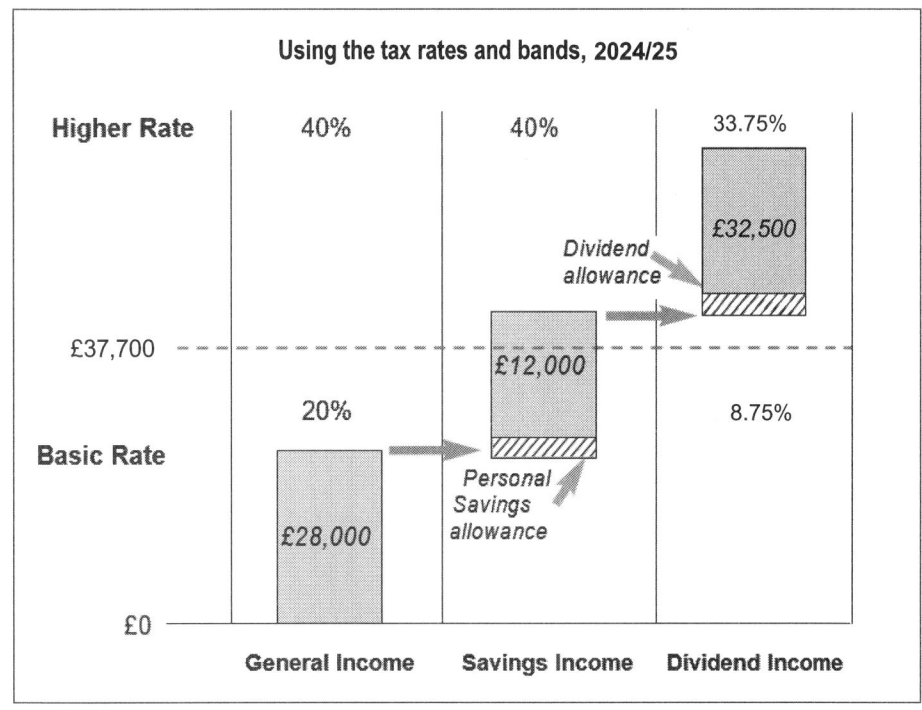

We can now use a Case Study to look at a more comprehensive Income Tax computation.

This Case Study does not refer to or use the Additional Rate band, since the taxable income is below £125,140. In Chapter 5 we will see how this band is used and also the impact of the changes to the personal allowance for those with high incomes.

Case Study

ANNE INVESTOR: INCOME TAX COMPUTATION

Anne Investor has the following income in 2024/25:
- Employment income of £28,000 from which £3,086 has been deducted in tax under PAYE
- Interest from bank and building society accounts totalling £16,250 (received gross)
- Dividends received of £22,000

Anne is entitled to the personal allowance of £12,570.

required

Using an Income Tax computation, calculate the Income Tax liability for 2024/25, and the amount of tax that has not yet been paid.

solution

Income Tax Computation

	Income £	Tax Paid £
Employment Income	28,000	3,086
Savings Income	16,250	0
Dividend Income	22,000	0
Total Income	66,250	3,086
less Personal Allowance	12,570	
Taxable Income	53,680	

Analysis of Taxable Income:

General Income (£28,000 – £12,570)	£15,430
Savings Income	£16,250
Dividend Income	£22,000
	£53,680

Income Tax Calculation:

	£	£
General Income:		
£15,430 x 20% (all in basic rate band)		3,086.00
Savings Income:		
£500 x 0% (personal savings allowance)	0.00	
£15,750 x 20% (all in basic rate band)	3,150.00	
£16,250		3,150.00
Dividend Income:		
£500 x 0% (dividend allowance)	0.00	
£5,520 x 8.75% (dividend ordinary rate)	483.00	
£15,980 x 33.75% (dividend upper rate)	5,393.25	
£22,000		5,876.25
Income Tax Liability		12,112.25
less Paid		3,086.00
Income Tax to be paid		9,026.25

income from savings and investments

The diagram below illustrates the situation

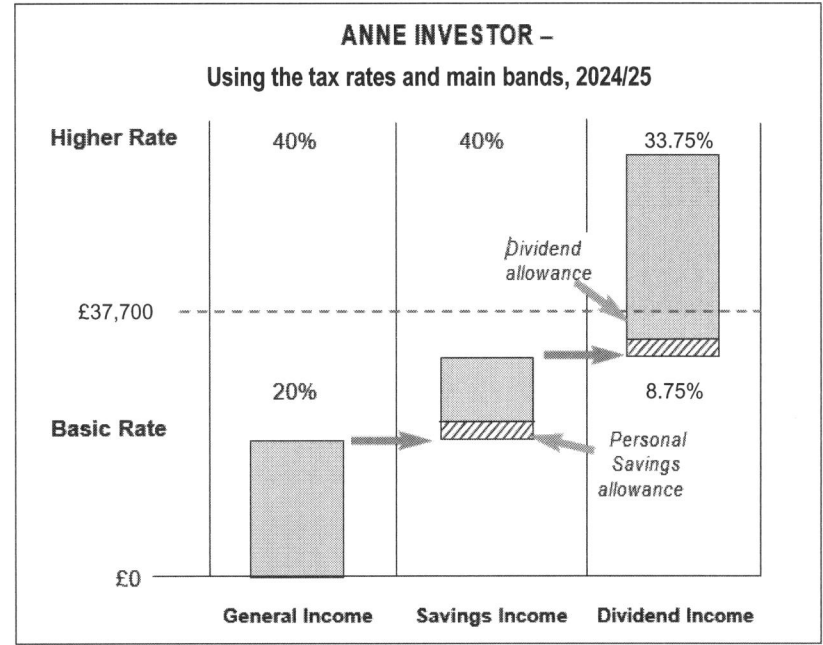

ASSESSMENT SUMMARY

As you can see, the Income Tax computation in the Case Study is more complicated than the calculations that we saw in the earlier chapters. The way the tax is calculated for each category of income by working up through the bands is illustrated in the chart shown above. Make sure that you can follow the logic, since it is very important for your success in this Unit that you can carry out computations like this accurately.

TAX-FREE INVESTMENT INCOME

Some specific types of investment income are exempt from Income Tax. You may recall that this was referred to in Chapter 1. The implications of having tax-free investment income are that:

- the tax-free income is not included in the Income Tax computation, and
- the tax-free income does not use up the personal savings allowance

individual savings accounts (ISAs)

You need to understand what individual savings accounts (ISAs) are and how they operate. These accounts provide income which is exempt from Income Tax. The accounts are also exempt from Capital Gains Tax.

Investment can be in 'stocks and shares' and/or 'cash' ISAs and/or 'innovative finance' ISAs, and are limited to a maximum total investment of £20,000 in 2024/25. There are no restrictions on how much can be invested in each category within this overall limit, and amounts invested in one category can subsequently be moved to the other.

For example, £20,000 could be invested in a 'stocks and shares ISA' in 2024/25, and subsequently some or all of it could be moved during the tax year to a 'cash ISA'. The same ability to move between cash and stocks and shares also applies to investments made in ISAs before this tax year.

There is no statutory minimum period of investment or minimum amount of investment in any type of ISA.

ISAs can only be held in one person's name – joint accounts are not permitted.

There are no limits on the number of different ISAs one can hold over time.

cash ISAs

Cash ISAs are effectively special accounts, mainly offered by banks or building societies. These accounts pay interest tax-free. Once an investment is made into an ISA, the income remains tax-free in subsequent tax years.

Usually, if a withdrawal is made from a cash ISA the amount cannot be reinvested without it counting as part of that year's maximum investment. Therefore if the maximum had already been invested, the withdrawn amount could not be reinvested during that tax year. An exception applies where the investment has been made in a **flexible ISA**. This type of ISA allows for reinvestment. This means that if some or all of the amount invested in a tax year is withdrawn during the tax year, it can be reinvested in the same tax year, without counting towards the maximum allowance for a second time.

Cash ISAs can be transferred to another provider (for example if interest rates are better), but this must be carried out by contacting the new provider who will organise the transfer. If an amount is simply withdrawn from an existing ISA account it will lose its tax-free status.

Investment in cash ISAs can be made by UK resident individuals who are aged 18 or over during the tax year.

stocks and shares ISAs and innovative finance ISAs

Stocks and shares ISAs are effectively tax-free 'wrappers' for investments including shares in listed companies and government securities (gilts).

Innovative finance ISAs can be used for peer-to-peer lending and crowdfunding debentures.

Investment in both these types of ISAs can be made by UK resident individuals who are aged 18 or over.

Chapter Summary

- Interest and dividends are categorised as 'Savings and Investment Income'. The basis of assessment is the gross amounts received in the tax year. Dividends are also received gross.

- Dividend income is taxed at different rates from general income. The rates for dividend income are 8.75%, 33.75% and 39.35%. Dividend income is considered the top slice of an individual's income, with savings income forming the next slice. This means that great care must be taken when calculating an individual's tax liability if income of these types is included.

- The personal savings allowance is available at up to £1,000 for basic rate taxpayers or up to £500 for higher rate taxpayers. The amount is used within the tax bands to charge Income Tax at 0% instead of the usual rate. Any excess over the allowance is subject to the normal rate of tax depending on the cumulative income. The allowance cannot be used against any other type of income.

- The dividend allowance of up to £500 is available to basic rate, higher rate and additional rate taxpayers. The amount is used within the tax bands to charge Income Tax at 0% instead of the usual rate. Any excess over the allowance is subject to the normal rate of tax depending on the cumulative income. The allowance cannot be used against any other type of income.

- Investment income from individual savings accounts (ISAs) is exempt from Income Tax. There are various rules concerning investments in ISAs.

Key Terms

savings and investment income — the term used to describe income that arises from the ownership of certain assets; it can include savings income and dividend income

personal savings allowance — an allowance that is used within the tax bands to provide tax-free savings income for basic rate and higher rate taxpayers of up to £1,000 or up to £500

dividends — these are the rewards received by investors in company shares; the amount is received gross

dividend allowance — an allowance that is used within the tax bands to provide tax-free dividend income of up to £500

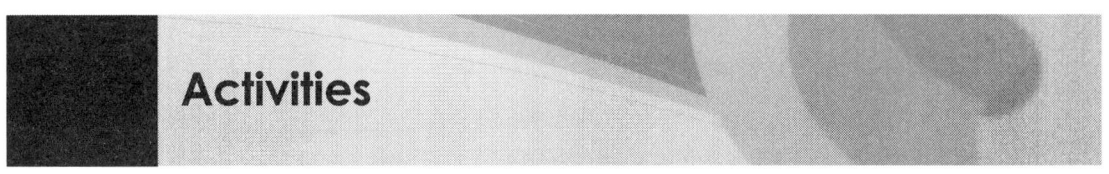

Activities

3.1 An individual has the following income in 2024/25, before deducting the personal allowance:

Employment income   £20,720
Savings income   £6,500

Select the total amount of Income Tax payable from the following options:

(a)	£5,300	
(b)	£5,100	
(c)	£2,830	
(d)	£2,730	
(e)	£1,630	

3.2 An individual has the following income in 2024/25 before deducting the personal allowance:

Employment income   £21,000
Savings Income   £1,300
Dividend income   £350

Calculate the amount of Income Tax that is payable on:

(a) savings income, and

(b) dividend income

3.3 Sophie had the following income in 2024/25:

Income from Employment (gross amount)	£29,150
Building Society Interest (amount received)	£1,500
Dividends from UK Companies (amount received)	£1,800
Property Income (agreed assessable amount)	£1,900

Sophie had Income Tax deducted under PAYE of £3,316. She is entitled to the personal allowance of £12,570.

Required:

Prepare Sophie's Income Tax Computation for the tax year, including calculations of her total Income Tax liability, and the part of this amount that has yet to be paid.

3.4 Brian had the following income in 2024/25:

Salary of £1,800 per month (gross) from his employment.

Dividends from UK companies (amount received)	£5,500
Bank Deposit Account Interest (amount received)	£2,000

Brian had £1,806 deducted under PAYE.

Required:

Prepare Brian's Income Tax Computation for the tax year, including calculations of his total Income Tax liability, and the part of this amount that has yet to be paid, or refunded.

3.5 Major Player had employment income of £25,650 (gross) in 2024/25, on which he paid £2,616 tax under PAYE. He has provided you with the following details of the amounts that he has received from his investments.

Date Received	Details	Amount Rec'd £
31/3/2024	Osborne Bank Deposit Account Interest	190.00
31/5/2024	Dividend from Growth plc	4,000.00
30/6/2024	Interest from 'gilt' (received gross)	1,500.00
30/9/2024	Interest from Nationside cash ISA	300.00
31/1/2025	Bank of Northumberland Deposit A/C Interest	11,875.00
31/3/2025	Osborne Bank Deposit Account Interest	750.00
30/6/2025	Dividend from Growth plc	1,600.00

Required:

(a) Produce schedules of the amounts of savings and dividend income assessable in the tax year.

(b) Prepare an Income Tax Computation for the tax year, including calculations of his total Income Tax liability, and the tax payable.

3.6 Individual savings accounts (ISAs) are subject to various rules. Select from the following, the rules that apply in 2024/25.

(a)	Cash ISAs and stocks and shares ISAs are subject to a maximum total investment in the tax year of £20,000	
(b)	Joint ISA accounts can be opened, but only by married couples	
(c)	ISAs can only be opened by individuals who are resident in the UK	
(d)	At the end of the tax year the tax-free status of investments made in a stocks and shares ISA expires	
(e)	The total invested in a stocks and shares ISA can subsequently be transferred to a cash ISA	

income from savings and investments 65

4 Income from employment

this chapter covers...

In this chapter we look in detail at one of the most important categories of personal tax – employment income.

We start by explaining the basis of assessment, and then discuss the difference between employment and being self-employed.

A major section in this chapter relates to benefits in kind. These are non-cash rewards for employees and the rules for calculating the assessable amounts are rather complicated. We will examine the rules that apply to company cars and their fuel, cheap loans, living accommodation and the provision of various other assets and benefits. We will also list benefits that are exempt from any tax charge.

We then move on to a section about expenses. These are payments that an employee makes in connection with his employment that may be reimbursed by his employer. We will examine the rules about when such expenses can be treated as an allowable deduction in the calculation of assessable employment income.

Finally we will see how to calculate National Insurance Contributions (NICs) relating to employees and employers.

THE BASIS OF ASSESSMENT FOR EMPLOYMENT INCOME

Income from employment is assessed under 'Employment, Pensions and Social Security Income', and the Income Tax is normally collected through Pay-As-You-Earn (PAYE). We will generally include this in the Income Tax computation simply as 'employment income'. The basis of assessment is:

	gross income **received** in the tax year
plus	the assessable value of any benefits in kind
less	any allowable deductions
equals	assessable income from employment

You will notice that (like savings and investment income) we are using a cash basis to determine which tax year any receipts are linked to, not an accruals basis. The period in which the income was earned may therefore not always be the one in which it is assessed; this could apply for example to commissions or bonuses that are earned in one period, but paid to the employee in a later one. You should therefore disregard any reference to the period in which employment income was earned, and concentrate just on when it was received. The only exception to this rule is the rare situation when an employee becomes entitled to income but chooses to receive it at a later date. In this case it is taxable in the tax year in which the employee is entitled to the income. As well as income from current employment, this category of income also includes pensions received and certain social security benefits.

employment and self-employment

The income from employment includes salaries, wages, bonuses, commissions, fees and gratuities (tips) where they relate to a job or office. It is important to distinguish between the concept of being employed (and having employment income) and being self-employed, the income from which is assessed as 'trading income'. Employment income results from an employment contract (even an implied one) where the employer exerts control over the employee. A self-employed person or contractor has much more control over the way he or she operates.

The distinction is whether the contract that applies is one of **service** (when the person is an **employee**), or a contract for services (a **self-employed** relationship). These can be confusing phrases, but if you think, a contract

- **of service** could apply to a servant (where the employee serves the employer)
- **for services** could apply to someone who invoices 'for services rendered' and is self-employed

In some cases it can be difficult to establish whether the person is employed or self-employed, and HMRC has produced leaflets and an online 'Employment Status Indicator' tool to help.

The following are indicators that help provide evidence in one direction or the other.

Indicators of Employment	Indicators of Self-Employment
Need to do the work yourself	Can employ helper or substitute
Told how, where and when to do work	Decide yourself how, when and where to do work
Work set hours and paid regular wage with sick pay and holidays	Choose work hours and invoice for work done
No risk of capital or losses	Risk own capital and bear losses from work that is not to standard
Employer provides equipment	Provide own equipment
Work for one employer (but sometimes more)	Work for several people or organisations

BENEFITS IN KIND

You will have noticed that employment income includes the assessable value of **benefits in kind**. This is the term used to describe any reward that an employee receives because of his employment that is not paid in money. It can therefore apply to a range of 'non-cash' items ranging from use of a company car to holidays paid for by the employer.

There are some situations where a payment on behalf of an employee may count as a benefit in kind, but the expense incurred would also be considered an **allowable deduction**, thereby cancelling out the effect of any tax charge. We will examine these situations in the 'allowable deductions' section later in this chapter.

Originally, benefits were assessed based on the cash cost to the employer of providing the employee with the benefit. While this rule is still used in some situations, there are now many types of benefit where specific rules are used to calculate the assessable amounts. Through this section we will now look at the more important benefits and how they are assessed. Although this is a complicated area, you must learn how to deal with all these examples, as they are popular examination topics.

company cars

A car owned (or leased) by the employer, but available for both business and private use by an employee is an assessable benefit. Most company cars have at least some private use, since the journey to and from work is considered private rather than business mileage. The way that the benefit is calculated is very specific, and is divided into two separate types of benefit:

- **a scale charge for having private use of the car** – the assessable amount is a percentage of the car's list price, and is deemed to include all the costs of the car, except fuel. It therefore includes road tax, insurance, repairs and servicing etc, and none of these costs are assessable separately
- **a scale charge for using fuel for private motoring** if this is paid for by the employer

We will describe the two benefits in turn.

scale charges for private use of cars

The scale charge for having use of the car depends on:

- the list price of the car when new
- the car's carbon dioxide emissions, measured in grams per kilometre (g/km)
- whether the car is petrol or diesel
- for some hybrid cars, what the pure electric range is

The system works by using percentages linked to emission levels (and sometimes the electric range). The appropriate percentage (up to 37%) is then applied to the list price of the car when new, and the result forms the assessable amount of the benefit. The higher the emissions, therefore, the higher the percentage and the higher the taxable benefit. The percentages change from time to time, since it is expected that typical emission levels will generally fall as new models are introduced.

For 2024/25 the charge for petrol or electric cars (or petrol-electric hybrid cars) works as follows:

- for cars with zero emissions (for example cars powered by only electricity) the charge is 2%
- for cars with emissions of 1 g/km to 50 g/km (for example petrol-electric hybrid cars) the charge is in the range 2% to 14% depending on the electric-only range
- for cars with emissions of 51 g/km to 54 g/km the charge is 15%
- for cars with emissions of 55 g/km to 59 g/km the charge is 16%
- for cars with emissions of 60 g/km to 64 g/km the charge is 17%
- for cars with emissions of 65 g/km to 69 g/km the charge is 18%

The system continues by increasing by 1% for every 5 g/km to a maximum of 37%, which applies to emissions of 160 g/km and over.

So, for example, cars with emissions of 105 g/km would have a charge of 26% of list price, and cars with emissions of 110 g/km would have a charge of 27%.

The easiest way to calculate the percentage for cars if the emissions are over 55 g/km is to:

- round the percentage down to a multiple of 5 (eg 149 would be rounded down to 145)
- work out how many steps of 5 g/km there are between your rounded figure and 55 g/km (eg (145 – 55) / 5 = 18)
- each of these steps represents an extra 1% that we add to the 16% that applies to emissions of 55 g/km (eg 16% + 18% = 34%)

example

If an employee is provided with a petrol engine car with a list price of £20,000, and an emission level of 153 g/km throughout 2024/25, then the assessable benefit would be calculated as:

Percentage: 16% + (1% x (150 – 55) / 5)

                = 16% + 19% = 35%.

The 35% is then multiplied by the list price of the car:

Benefit: £20,000 x 35% = £7,000

Cars that have an emissions level from 1 g/km to 50 g/km (inclusive) are typically hybrid cars with both electric and conventional engines. For cars with these emission levels, the electric only range (in miles) is also taken into account when determining the percentage that applies, as follows:

- a range of 130 miles or more results in a charge of 2%
- a range of 70 to 129 miles results in a charge of 5%
- a range of 40 to 69 miles results in a charge of 8%
- a range of 30 to 39 miles results in a charge of 12%
- a range of less than 30 miles results in a charge of 14%

This data (along with other relevant tax tables) is provided in pop-up form in your examination, and this is reproduced in the appendix at the back of this book.

The percentages that apply to cars powered solely by diesel are sometimes 4% more than those for petrol powered cars.

There is an exception to this 4% addition for diesel cars. This occurs where the car conforms to the 'Real Driving Emissions Step 2 (RDE2)' standard and was registered after 1/9/2017. If this applies to a diesel car then there is no addition to the scale charge that applies to petrol cars. Unless you are specifically told that a car meets the RDE2 standard you should assume that it does not, and therefore the 4% addition should be applied in your calculation.

Both petrol and diesel cars are subject to a maximum percentage of 37%.

example

If an employee is provided with a diesel engine car (that does not conform to RDE2) with a list price of £15,000, and an emission level of 137 grams per kilometre throughout 2024/25, then the assessable benefit would be:

£15,000 x (16% + 16% + 4% = 36%) = £5,400

You will need to remember how to carry out the calculations for electric, petrol, hybrid and diesel cars.

The figure calculated is adjusted in the following circumstances:

- where the car is not available to the employee for the whole tax year, the assessable amount is time-apportioned – this is a common adjustment in examination tasks. Note that for a period of time to count when the car is 'unavailable' it must be a continuous period of 30 days or more. So, for example, if a car could not be used because it was being repaired for 25 days then there would be no time-apportionment
- where the employee makes a **revenue** contribution to the employer for the use of the car, this is deducted from the assessable amount that would otherwise apply
- where the employee makes a **capital** contribution towards the cost of the car, this contribution, up to a maximum of £5,000, is deducted from the list price before the appropriate percentage is applied
- where accessories or modifications are added to the car before or at the time that the car is first made available to the employee, their cost is added to the list price. This would not apply, however, to equipment to enable a disabled person to use the car, nor to equipment which is necessary for the use of the car in the performance of the employee's duties (for example a tow bar if the employee was required to tow a trailer for his job). There is also an exception for the provision of special security equipment (e.g. bullet resistant glass) where it is necessary due to the employee's role

- where accessories are added to the car later on, these are added to the list price and applied to the whole tax year in which they were added. This only applies, however, to accessories that cost more than £100 each (or per set)
- where the company car is a 'classic' car over 15 years old at the end of the tax year and has a market value which is both over £15,000 and exceeds the list price, then the market value is used instead of the list price
- where an employee is provided with a chauffeur in addition to a company car, the cost of the chauffeur forms an additional assessable benefit

example

An employee was provided with a diesel engine company car (not RDE2 compliant) for the whole of 2024/25. The list price of the car was £25,000, and emissions were 123 g/km. The employee made a capital contribution towards the cost of the car of £7,000. In September 2024 the company paid for a set of 4 alloy wheels for the car. They cost £95 each.

The list price would be increased by the cost of the set of alloy wheels of £380 (applicable for the whole tax year), and there would be a deduction from the list price relating to the employee's capital contribution, but this would be limited to £5,000. The assessable benefit would therefore be:

£20,380 x (16% + 13% + 4% = 33%) = £6,725 (rounded)

fuel benefit for private use of company cars

When an employee is provided with a company car, the employer may agree to pay for the fuel (petrol or diesel) that the employee uses for private mileage as well as for business use. If this happens, a further assessable benefit arises, calculated as follows:

In **2024/25** the same percentage as is applied to the car (based on its emissions) is multiplied by a fixed amount of £27,800.

example

If an employee is provided with a petrol engine car with a list price of £20,000, and an emission level of 137 g/km throughout 2024/25, then the assessable **fuel benefit** would be:

£27,800 x 32% = £8,896 (by applying the emission percentage to the fixed amount of £27,800).

The fuel charge is time-apportioned if the car, for which private fuel is provided, is not available for the whole tax year. The same rule regarding a car being unavailable for at least 30 days applies to fuel as well as use of the car. Note however that the same fuel charge applies if the employee has **any** fuel provided for private mileage, no matter how little or how much. Unlike the car benefit itself, the employee making a contribution to the employer will have no effect on the assessable benefit for fuel. The only way for an employee to avoid the charge is to pay privately (or reimburse the employer) for **all** private fuel that has been used.

Note that for cars that run exclusively on electricity (and have 0% g/km CO_2) there is no fuel benefit charge.

pool cars

Pool cars are cars whose use is shared amongst employees for business purposes. There is no assessable benefit for employees who use pool cars, but the definition of a pool car is strict. To qualify as a non-assessable pool car it must:

- be primarily used for business purposes and any private use must be incidental
- be used by several employees, and
- not normally be kept at an employee's home

vans

Where an employer provides a small van that can be used privately, there is a scale charge. The assessable benefit for 2024/25 is £3,960. This amount does not include any private fuel, which is assessed separately – currently based on an amount of £757 per year. Where the employee uses the van privately only for travel between home and work and insignificant other private use, this will not be classed as a benefit.

If a van is 'zero-emission' (for example powered solely by electricity) then the assessable benefit for private use is zero and there is no assessable benefit for fuel in the form of electricity.

cheap (or 'beneficial') loans

Where a loan is granted to an employee and charged at less than the HM Revenue & Customs official interest rate, there may be an assessable benefit.

This official rate was 2.25% pa at the time that this book was published. This rate does change from time to time. You will be provided with the current official rate in an examination through the pop-up reference material, which must be used to gain maximum marks.

The benefit is calculated as the difference between the interest charge that would be generated by using the official rate, and the actual interest charged. However, there is no assessable benefit if the loan (or total loans) outstanding is £10,000 or less throughout the tax year 2024/25.

There is also no assessable benefit for a loan (of any amount) that is used entirely to purchase equipment (but not cars etc) for wholly business use.

If a loan (of any amount) is written off by the employer then the whole amount is assessable.

example

An employer provides his employee with a £20,000 loan at an interest rate of 1% per year.

The actual interest charge would be £200 per year, assuming no capital repayments.

The assessable benefit would therefore be (£20,000 x 2.25%) minus £200 = £250.

The above example was based on a simple situation where the same amount was outstanding for the whole tax year. Where examples are more complex, with part repayments or additional loans being made, there are two calculation methods which HMRC will accept:

- the first method is to calculate **exactly** the interest figures based on the balances owed for each proportion of the year
- the second is a simple **average** method which we will explain below. This is the method that you will be expected to use in your examination where necessary

The following method is used to work out the assessable benefit of a single loan. If there were more than one loan, the method would be applied to each loan and the final results added together.

- start with the loan balance at either the start of the tax year or the start of the loan if later
- add the loan balance at either the end of the tax year or just before the loan ended if earlier
- divide the total of these figures by 2
- time-apportion this based on complete months of the loan (eg 6/12 for a loan that was only held for 6 months in the tax year)
- multiply this by the difference between the official interest rate (currently 2.25%) and the rate paid (if any)

> **example**
>
> John was granted a loan from his employer of £15,000 on 1 January 2024 at an interest rate of 0.5%. John repaid £4,000 on 1 July 2024, and then repaid the remaining £11,000 on 6 January 2025.
>
> | | |
> |---|---:|
> | Balance at start of tax year 2024/25 (since the loan was taken out before this) | £15,000 |
> | Balance just before repayment (since this occurred before the end of the tax year) | £11,000 |
> | | £26,000 |
> | | ÷ 2 = £13,000 |
>
> £13,000 x 9/12 (months of loan in this tax year) x (2.25% – 0.5%) = £170 (rounded down)
>
> The assessable amount will be £170.
>
> Note that in this example the date of the partial repayment was not relevant.

living accommodation

Where the employer provides free accommodation for an employee, this can result in an assessable benefit. Unless an exemption applies (as we will see later in this section), the assessable benefit works as follows:

- the assessable amount for the accommodation itself is normally the **higher** of the 'annual value' (based on the rateable value), and the rent paid by the employer (if the property is not owned by the employer)
- where the accommodation was purchased by the employer, and cost more than £75,000, then an additional assessment is applied. This is based on the excess of the purchase price over £75,000 multiplied by the HM Revenue & Customs official interest rate. This is the same rate (currently 2.25%) that is used to calculate the benefit of cheap loans as described above. See later for accommodation purchased more than six years before the employee first moves in
- the cost figure is increased by any capital expenditure incurred on the property between the date of purchase and the start of the current tax year. Any capital expenditure during the current tax year is therefore ignored for this year's calculation, but will be used in the following tax year
- the cost of any other living expenses paid by the employer would be added to the assessment (for example electricity costs). Furniture and other assets provided by the employer will also result in an assessable benefit as we will see in the next section

- if an employee does not have use of the accommodation for the whole tax year, then any assessable benefit (as described above) would be time-apportioned
- any rent or similar amount paid by the employee to the employer for use of the accommodation is deducted from the benefit figure calculated

example

An employee is allowed to live in a company flat free of charge throughout the tax year. The annual value of the flat is £1,500, and the employer also pays the heating costs of the flat which amount to £600 per year.

The flat cost the employer £100,000 when it was originally purchased, 3 years ago.

Assuming that the employee could not claim any exemption from the flat being assessable, the amount would be calculated as follows:

Annual value	£1,500
Additional charge (£100,000 – £75,000) x 2.25%	£562
Other expenses paid by employer	£600
Total assessable benefit	£2,662

If the accommodation was only available to the employee for 6 months of the tax year, the benefit would be £2,662 x 6/12 = £1,331.

When accommodation is provided which was purchased by the employer more than **six years** before the date that the employee first moves in, the following applies: the **market value when first occupied by the employee** is used in the calculation of additional charge instead of the purchase price (before the standard £75,000 is deducted).

Where there have been capital improvements to the property between the date of purchase and the start of the current tax year, these will be ignored if the market value being used is based on a date after the improvements were made. This is logical since otherwise the value of the improvements would be double counted.

The following examples will illustrate two situations.

- a house is first provided to an employee on 1 September 2024. On that date the market value of the house was £400,000. The house was purchased by the employer on 30 June 2019 for £280,000 and in August 2019 an extension was added costing £50,000.

In this case the market value **is not** used in the calculation since the period 30 June 2019 to 1 September 2024 is **less than 6 years**. The additional charge will therefore be calculated using the purchase price plus the cost of the extension, and is based on 7 months occupation in 2024/25.

Additional charge:

(£280,000 + £50,000 – £75,000) x 2.25% x 7/12 = £3,346 (rounded down)

- a house is first provided to an employee on 1 September 2024. On that date the market value of the house was £400,000. The house was purchased by the employer on 30 June 2018 for £280,000 and in August 2019 an extension was added costing £50,000.

In this case the market value **is** used in the calculation since the period 30 June 2018 to 1 September 2024 is **more than 6 years**. The additional charge will therefore be calculated using the market value (and ignoring the cost of the extension), and is based on 7 months occupation in 2024/25.

Additional charge:

(£400,000 – £75,000) x 2.25% x 7/12 = £4,265 (rounded down)

job-related accommodation

For the accommodation itself to result in no assessable benefit, one of the following situations must apply:

- the employee is a representative occupier (for example a caretaker)
- it is customary to provide the employee with accommodation in that particular job (for example a vicar)
- the accommodation is provided for security reasons

These situations are sometimes referred to as 'job-related accommodation'.

Note that in these situations the annual value and additional charge for properties over £75,000 is not applied. However, any running expenses of the accommodation (except council tax and water charges) that are paid for by the employer will still result in an assessable benefit. In these circumstances the benefit of such costs will be restricted to a maximum of 10% of the employee's earnings from the job.

provision of other assets

Where an asset is given to an employee then the assessable benefit is the market value of the asset at that time. Apart from vehicles, if an asset is provided for an employee's private use (but remains belonging to the employer) then there is an assessable benefit of 20% of the market value of the asset when first provided.

If the asset that the employee has private use of is rented or hired by the employer (instead of owned) then the assessable benefit is the **higher** of:

- 20% of the market value when first provided, and
- the rental or hire charge paid by the employer

This benefit would apply to each tax year that it was used by the employee.

If an asset that was provided in this way is subsequently given to the employee (or he/she buys it from the employer) then a further benefit may arise based on the higher of:

- market value at the date of the transfer, and
- market value when first provided, less benefits for use of the asset already assessed

From the higher of these figures is deducted any amount paid by the employee.

example

An employee is provided with the use of a home entertainment system, when its market value was £1,000. Two years later he buys it from the employer, paying £100, when its market value was £300.

The benefit assessed for each year that it was owned by the employer and the employee used it would be £1,000 x 20% = £200.

The benefit assessed upon purchase would be the higher of:

- market value at the date of the transfer (£300), and
- market value when first provided, less benefits assessed already (£1,000 – £200 – £200 = £600)

i.e. £600, minus amount paid by the employee of £100 = £500

These calculations would also apply to furniture owned by the employer in accommodation used by an employee.

vouchers, credit cards, and other benefits paid by the employer

Where an employee is provided with a voucher that can be spent in a specified way, the benefit is the cost to the employer of providing the voucher. This may be less than the face value of the voucher.

For example, suppose an employer gave his employee a £500 voucher at Christmas to spend in a particular store. If the voucher cost the employer £470 then this amount would be the assessable benefit.

If an employee has use of a company credit card, then any expenditure will be assessable, except:

- business expenditure that qualifies as an allowable deduction (see next section), and
- expenditure on benefits that are assessed separately (for example in connection with a company car or its fuel)

Where an employer provides an employee with goods or services for private use, the cost to the employer is the assessable amount. This could arise if an employer paid for a holiday for an employee, or paid their train fare from home to work.

tax-free benefits

The following is a summary of the main benefits that are not taxable – ie that are excluded from the benefits included in assessable employment income. Some of these have already been mentioned earlier in this chapter:

- use of 'zero-emission' van (but not car)
- electricity to fuel a 'zero-emission' car or van
- use of a van provided by the employer, provided the only non-business use is travel from home to work and other insignificant private mileage
- childcare provided by the employer – for example, a workplace creche
- an allowance to cover incidental expenses while working away from home of up to £5 per night while in the UK and £10 per night while overseas
- workplace parking
- job-related accommodation
- a loan from the employer at a low, or nil rate of interest, providing the loan does not exceed £10,000 at any time during the tax year or is to purchase equipment entirely for business use
- meals at a staff canteen – provided it is available to all staff
- in-house sports facilities (not facilities available to the general public)

- up to one health screening assessment and one medical check up in any year
- free eye checks and spectacles for employees with significant use of display screen equipment (DSE) at work
- employers' contributions to pension schemes
- mobile telephone provided by employer (including cost of calls) – limited to one per employee
- an allowance of £6 per week (or £26 per month) to cover expenses incurred by employees required by their employer to work at home
- goodwill gifts for an employee (goods or voucher for goods) that are provided by someone other than the employer (and not connected with the employer), restricted to a cost of £250 or less
- payment of a qualifying award under a staff suggestion scheme – up to a maximum of £5,000
- long service awards to employees with 20 years or more service (and there has been no similar award in the previous 10 years), based on a value of up to £50 per year of service; the award can be in the form of shares or a tangible asset
- relocation costs of up to £8,000 on a change of residence due to a change in the place of work
- costs of annual staff parties which are open to staff generally and cost no more than £150 per head
- scholarships paid to employees who attend a full-time course for at least one academic year at a recognised educational establishment. The amount paid is tax free up to £15,480 per academic year, provided it does not relate to working for the employer during vacations
- reimbursement of expenses that are incurred on behalf of the employer, or that are an allowable deduction – see next section

trivial benefits in kind

In addition to the exempt benefits listed above, there is also exemption from tax for 'trivial benefits' that meet all the following conditions:

- the cost per employee does not **exceed £50** (or the average cost if it is impractical to calculate the exact cost per employee)
- the benefit is **not** cash or a cash voucher
- the employee is **not entitled** to the benefit as part of a contractual obligation

- the benefit is **not** in recognition of the employee's performance of their duties

The exemption also applies to the benefits provided to an employee's family.

Examples of trivial benefits that **would be exempt** from tax (provided costing less than £50) include:

- taking an employee out for a meal on their birthday
- giving an employee a gift at Christmas (not related to their performance)
- giving an employee a non-cash voucher on the birth of their child
- sending flowers to a sick employee

Examples that **would not be exempt** from tax include:

- a benefit costing more than £50; this would be wholly taxable – not just the excess
- a gift in recognition of hitting performance targets; this is wholly taxable

Where a benefit could be covered under either these rules or a specific rule mentioned earlier, the most favourable position for the employee can apply. For example, if an employer provided two annual functions for employees, one costing £140 each and another costing £40 each, both could be exempt as follows. The £140 function would be covered by the £150 limit on exempt staff parties mentioned earlier. The £40 function could then be treated as an exempt trivial benefit.

BENNY FITT:
EMPLOYMENT INCOME INCLUDING BENEFITS IN KIND

Benny Fitt works as a Sales Manager for ESP Limited. He was employed throughout 2024/25 at a basic salary of £25,000 per year, plus a six-monthly bonus dependent on his performance. He received the following bonus payments:

Period related to bonus	Amount	Date Received
July - Dec 2023	£2,000	28/2/24
Jan - June 2024	£2,400	31/8/24
July - Dec 2024	£2,700	28/2/25
Jan - June 2025	£3,000	31/8/25

He was provided with a diesel engine car, not RDE2 compliant with a list price of £25,500 and an emission rating of 192 g/km from the beginning of the tax year until 5 December.

After that date the car was exchanged for a new petrol engine car with a list price of £15,000 and an emission rating of 119 g/km, which was kept until after the end of the tax year. Benny was provided with free fuel for private purposes for both cars.

He was granted an interest-free loan of £12,000 by ESP Limited on 6/4/24. He had not made any repayments by 5/4/25.

Benny was also provided with a home cinema system on 6/4/23 with a value of £800 at that time. On 6/4/24 he bought the system from the company for £250, when its second-hand value was £400.

required

Calculate the assessable amount of employment income for Benny for the tax year 2024/25. Assume that the HM Revenue & Customs official interest rate is 2.25% throughout the year.

solution

salary and bonuses:

The date that the money was received determines which tax year it is assessed in. This gives the following figures for 2024/25:

		£
Basic Salary		25,000
Bonuses –	rec'd 31 August 24	2,400
	rec'd 28 Feb 25	2,700
		30,100

The other bonuses are assessed before or after the year that we are concerned with.

company cars

The assessable benefit of each car is calculated separately, based on the proportion of the tax year that it is provided.

Car one is based on a percentage of (16% + 27% + 4%) = 47%, but limited to 37%.

The assessable benefit for this car is therefore:

37% x £25,500 x 8/12 =	£6,290

Car two is based on a percentage of 28% (16% + 12%).
The assessable benefit for this car is therefore:

28% x £15,000 x 4/12 =	£1,400
Total company car benefit	£7,690

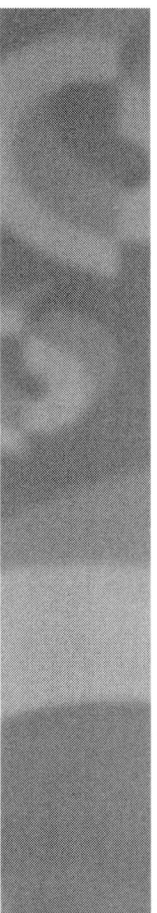

car fuel

Car one: 37% x £27,800 x 8/12 =	£6,857
Car two: 28% x £27,800 x 4/12 =	£2,594
Total car fuel benefit	£9,451

interest-free loan

Since the full amount is outstanding throughout the year, and no interest is charged, the benefit is based on the amount lent multiplied by the official rate.

£12,000 x 2.25%   £270

home cinema

In the first year (2023/24) 20% of the value is charged (£160). In the second year (2024/25) the charge is based on the original value less previous benefit, since this is greater than the second-hand value.

(£800 – £160) minus £250 paid by Benny   £390

Employment Income Summary

	£
Salary & Bonuses	30,100
Company Cars	7,690
Car Fuel	9,451
Loan	270
Home Cinema	390
Employment income assessable amount	47,901

ALLOWABLE DEDUCTIONS

We will now examine the amounts that can be deducted from the income and benefits received in respect of employment, and therefore reduce the employment income assessment. These are specific amounts that the employee has paid out in connection with the employment.

The general rule is that to be allowable against employment income, expenditure must be incurred **wholly, exclusively and necessarily** in the performance of the duties of the employment. You may recognise part of this phrase from our studies of property income; but here the word 'necessarily' is added. This means that strictly speaking, allowable expenditure must be for something that the employment duties could not be carried out without – not just that the job is carried out more easily or efficiently because of the expenditure. For example, personal clothing is not an allowable deduction, even if it was bought especially for work and only worn to work. There are specific instances where expenditure is allowable outside this stringent test, but you should use this basic rule when you come across expenditure that you are unsure how to treat.

expenditure reimbursed by the employer

Where an employee's expenditure is reimbursed by the employer, if the original expenditure is allowable, then the reimbursement is exempt from tax. This means that the expenditure and the reimbursement effectively cancel each other out and there is no impact on tax.

If, however, the expenditure being reimbursed is not specifically allowable, or does not meet the 'wholly, exclusively and necessarily' rule then the reimbursement will be taxable.

We will now look at how to deal with some specific types of expenditure. These items may or may not be reimbursed by an employer.

using your own transport for business

This relates to travelling within the job (eg journeys from one site to another), not for travelling from home to the normal workplace (which counts as private motoring). HM Revenue & Customs has published mileage rates that constitute allowable expenditure as follows:

Cars and vans:	First 10,000 miles in tax year	45p per mile
	Additional mileage	25p per mile
Motor cycles		24p per mile
Bicycles:		20p per mile

Note that this does not apply to company cars – only for use of the employees' own transport. It may well be that the employer reimburses a mileage allowance. Where this is exactly in line with these figures, the benefit received cancels out the allowable expenditure, but if it is at a higher rate, the excess is a net taxable benefit. If the rates paid by the employer are lower (or expenses are not reimbursed at all) then the shortfall is a net allowable deduction. This system is known as 'Approved Mileage Allowance Payments' (AMAP).

entertaining and subsistence

Where an employee incurs expenditure on the costs of spending time away from his/her normal place of work, these costs are normally allowable. Entertaining of the employer's clients is only allowable if the employer has reimbursed the employee, and then the benefit will not be chargeable.

professional fees & subscriptions

Where an employee pays a professional fee or subscription to an organisation that is relevant to his or her employment, the cost is an allowable expense. HM Revenue & Customs has a list of approved bodies (available on its website), and the AAT is amongst the accountancy bodies on the list. Where the employer pays the subscription for the employee, the benefit received is cancelled out by the allowable deduction.

pension contributions

Contributions that an employee makes to an approved company pension scheme are allowable deductions within employment income. If the contributions are made to a scheme run by the employer, then the deduction will often be made automatically before PAYE is operated on the balance of income. If this is the situation, then amounts shown on an employee's P45 and P60 will represent income after the employee's pension contribution has been deducted. You may recall that the employer's contribution to an approved pension scheme is not taxable as a part of an employee's income, so the employee gains two advantages if both he/she and his/her employer contribute to such a scheme. If an employer makes contributions into a pension scheme, but the employee does not contribute, this is known as a 'non-contributory' pension scheme.

payroll giving scheme

Where an arrangement has been made between an employer and an approved Payroll Giving Agency, employees can authorise deductions (without limit) through the payroll of donations to charities. This is allowed as a deduction from earnings, and the employer is able to operate PAYE on the income after the donation has been deducted – just like employees' pension contributions. The employee therefore gets tax relief on his/her donations, and the employer passes the gross amount of the donations onto the Payroll Giving Agency, and this organisation distributes the amounts to the named charities.

Case Study

AL LOWE:
BENEFITS AND ALLOWABLE DEDUCTIONS

Al is employed as an administrator by Spencer & Company, and is paid a gross salary of £22,000 per year. He makes a contribution of 5% of his salary to the company pension scheme (a scheme that is approved by HM Revenue & Customs). Spencer & Company also pays a contribution into the pension fund of 8% of Al's salary.

As a bonus, he was given vouchers to spend on a holiday with a particular travel agent. The retail value of the vouchers was £1,500, and these cost Spencer & Company £1,350.

Al is required to undertake business journeys in his own car, for which the company agreed to reimburse him at a rate of 55p per mile. Al used his car for 7,500 business miles during the tax year, and the company paid him the agreed amounts. He also claimed £300 for subsistence allowances while away on company business, and this was also paid to him. The subsistence payments are incurred wholly, exclusively and necessarily in the performance of Al's duties.

Al pays an annual subscription to the Association of Administrative Managers (a professional body, approved by HM Revenue & Customs). This amounted to £140. Spencer & Company did not reimburse him for this.

Al also pays £30 per month to Oxfam under the 'payroll giving scheme' organised by Spencer & Company. This amount is deducted each month from his salary.

required

Calculate the assessable amount of employment income for Al for the tax year.

solution

	£
Gross Salary	22,000
less	
5% pension contribution	(1,100)
payroll giving scheme	(360)
Amount used for PAYE purposes	20,540
add benefits:	
Mileage paid in excess of HMRC approved rate	
7,500 × (55p − 45p)	750
Cost of holiday vouchers	1,350
less allowable deduction:	
Professional fee paid	(140)
Assessable amount	22,500

Note that:

- the employer's contribution to the pension scheme is not included as a benefit
- the subsistence allowance is the reimbursement of an allowable cost, so does not need to be considered further

REDUNDANCY PAYMENTS

Redundancy payments (compensation for loss of employment) are not strictly emoluments, nor are they benefits in kind. The types of redundancy payments, and the rules regarding whether they are taxable, can be very complex. Generally the first £30,000 of a redundancy payment is exempt from Income Tax.

NATIONAL INSURANCE CONTRIBUTIONS

We will now turn our attention to National Insurance Contributions (NICs) as they affect employees and employers. The first category that we will examine is known as NIC Class 1 contributions, and depends on the level of the employee's pay. The contributions are collected through the payroll under PAYE. Although there are some technical terms to be understood, the calculations are generally quite straightforward.

employee (primary) rates

The amounts of NIC paid by employees are known as primary contributions. There are various NI categories of employees, which are labelled with letters. The most common category is A, which relates to most employees, and we will use this to illustrate the calculation of NIC. We will explain exactly which employees fall into each category a little later.

Employees in category A will pay **primary contributions** as follows:

- earnings above the Primary Threshold (PT) up to and including the Upper Earnings Limit (UEL) are charged at 8%
- the balance of earnings above the Upper Earnings Limit (UEL) is charged at 2%

Employees with earnings at or below the Primary Threshold (PT) do not pay any contributions.

The Primary Threshold and Upper Earnings Limit can be expressed as weekly, monthly, or annual amounts. The NICs calculation will normally be based on one of these, depending on how frequently the employee is paid. The calculations are not carried out on cumulative pay amounts throughout the tax year, except for Directors as we will see later. The figures are as follows for 2024/25:

	Per Week	Per Month	Per Year
Primary Threshold (PT)	£242	£1,048	£12,570
Upper Earnings Limit (UEL)	£967	£4,189	£50,270

You will notice that the annual Upper Earnings Limit is the same at the point at which employees with no other income would become higher rate taxpayers, based on Personal Allowance of £12,570 plus Basic Rate Band of £37,700.

The following examples will illustrate the calculation of employees' primary NIC.

example

Brian has weekly pay of £300.

He will pay NIC of (£300 – £242) × 8% = £4.64 per week.

Anna has weekly pay of £1,000.

She will pay NIC of:

(£967 – £242) × 8%   = £58.00, plus

(£1,000 – £967) × 2%   = £0.66, making a total of £58.66 per week.

Rashid has monthly pay of £5,000.

He will pay NIC of:

(£4,189 – £1,048) × 8%   = £251.28, plus

(£5,000 – £4,189) × 2%   = £16.22 making a total of £267.50 per month.

You could be asked to calculate NIC using weekly, monthly or annual figures. You will be provided with the appropriate data.

Employees earning below the Primary Threshold will not pay any NIC. However, if they earn at or above the Lower Earnings Level (LEL), but below the Primary Threshold, they will be credited with making contributions at 0%. This will then count towards their entitlement to state pensions and other benefits. The Lower Earnings Limit is currently £123 per week, the equivalent of £6,396 per year.

employer (secondary) rates

While employees pay primary NIC as a deduction from their pay, employers pay their secondary NIC as an additional cost of employing each individual. Payment is made by the employer to HMRC on a monthly basis, together with the Income Tax and employees' NIC that has been deducted from employees.

We will again use **category A** employees to illustrate the calculations of the employer's contributions.

Employers will pay **secondary contributions** based on employee earnings as follows:

- all earnings above the Secondary Threshold (ST) without limit are charged at **13.8%**

Notice that there is no upper limit for secondary contributions.

The Secondary Threshold is as follows for 2024/25:

	Per Week	Per Month	Per Year
Secondary Threshold (ST)	£175	£758	£9,100

For this tax year you will notice that the Secondary Threshold figures are different to the Primary Threshold ones.

We will use the earlier examples to illustrate the calculation of employers' secondary NIC.

example

Brian has weekly pay of £300.

His employer will pay NIC of:

(£300 – £175) x 13.8% = £17.25 per week.

Anna has weekly pay of £1,000.

Her employer will pay NIC of:

(£1,000 – £175) x 13.8% = £113.85 per week.

Rashid has monthly pay of £5,000.

His employer will pay NIC of:

(£5,000 – £758) x 13.8% = £585.39 per month.

'earnings' for Class 1 NIC purposes

The earnings figure that is used to calculate employees' and employers' **Class 1** contributions are similar to those 'cash' payments (excluding benefits in kind) used for Income Tax purposes.

However, there are two significant differences, where amounts are deducted from employees' pay (for tax purposes) relating to:

- contributions to approved company pension schemes, and/or
- payroll giving schemes

Neither of these deductions are taken into account for NIC purposes and the NIC calculations are made based on the gross pay before these amounts are taken off.

Cash expense payments that are not taxable are generally not subject to Class 1 NIC. However, where expenses are paid that are taxable (for example mileage payments in excess of AMAP rates), these will be subject to NIC.

NIC for directors

Where company directors are paid as employees, NIC employees' and employers' contributions will apply. The following special rules apply to the NIC calculation.

Directors' NIC must either be calculated on a cumulative basis throughout the tax year, or can be calculated as normal for each pay day, but a year-end check carried out on a cumulative basis. If the cumulative NIC at the year-end results in a higher figure then this will apply.

If the same amount has been paid to the director each pay day then there will be no significant difference in the two figures. However, where the amounts paid each period are very different, there can be large differences. The system exists to prevent directors manipulating their pay receipts to minimise the NIC liability.

The following example will illustrate this situation.

example

Sophie is a director of a limited company that pays her as an employee. She received £650 per month for 11 months of the tax year, and £20,000 for the final month. Her total annual pay is £27,150.

Using the payment by payment calculation, there would be no NIC (employees' or employers') for the first 11 months. In the 12th month the employees' NIC would be:

((£4,189 – £1,048) x 8%) + ((£20,000 – 4,189) x 2%) = £567.50

This would be compared with the calculation for the year as a whole, as if it has been paid in one amount.

(£27,150 – £12,570) x 8% = £1,166.40

Sophie's employees' NIC contribution in the last month would therefore be increased to £1,166.40. The employers' contribution would be calculated using the same procedure.

If Sophie had not been a director, her total employees' NIC for the year would have been £567.50. However, it is unlikely that the employment contract for a normal employee would specify such an extreme payment structure.

employers' Class 1A NIC

So far in this section we have considered Class 1 NIC. As just noted these relate to earnings excluding benefits in kind. **Class 1A contributions** are only made by **employers**, and relate to the taxable value of **benefits in kind** provided to employees.

Class 1A NIC is paid annually by employers and forms an additional cost of providing benefits in kind. There is no equivalent NIC charge for employees.

The rate of Class 1A employers' NIC is 13.8% – the same rate as the main rate for cash earnings. There is no threshold equivalent to the Secondary Threshold applicable to Class 1A.

---

example

Rashid was provided with a petrol company car and all fuel throughout 2024/25. The car had a list price of £28,000, and CO_2 emissions of 95 g/km.

The taxable benefit would be as follows:

Use of car	24% × £28,000 =	£6,720
Fuel	24% × £27,800 =	£6,672
Total		£13,392

The Class 1A NIC payable by Rashid's employer after the end of the tax year would be (£13,392 × 13.8%) = £1,848.09.

There would be no additional NIC payable by Rashid on the benefit.

NIC employment allowance

For 2024/25 employers can reduce the amount of **employers' NIC** by up to £5,000 by claiming the **employment allowance**. This can be claimed by most employers, with the exception of companies with only one director/employee. Where the total employers' NIC for the tax year is less than £5,000 then it will be reduced to zero by the allowance, and where the total is more than £5,000 it will be reduced by £5,000.

employees not in category A

So far in our studies of NIC we have examined category A employees, who make up the vast majority of employees.

The following employees do not pay **NIC on their earnings:**

- individuals under the age of 16 (classed as category X)
- individuals over pensionable age (classed as category C)

However, **employers of category C** employees are required to pay secondary NIC at the same rates as for category A employees.

There are also special rates for **employers' contributions** relating to the following categories of employees:

Category H   Apprentices under the age of 25

Category M   Employees under the age of 21

However, category H and M employees pay the same primary rates as category A employees.

If you are asked to calculate NIC for any category of employee, you will be provided with data on the rates and thresholds.

income from employment

Chapter Summary

- Income from employment is categorised as 'Income from Employment, Pensions and Social Security'. The basis of assessment is the gross income received in the tax year, plus the assessable value of any benefits in kind, less any allowable deductions. Employers are required to operate the PAYE system whereby tax is deducted from payments made to employees throughout the tax year.

- Benefits in kind are generally assessed on the cost to the employer of providing the benefit. However, many more specific rules have been developed to calculate the assessable amount of certain benefits.

- Company cars that are available for an employee's private use have an assessable amount based on a percentage of the list price of the car. The percentage will depend on the carbon dioxide emission rating of the car, when it was first registered, and whether it has an electric, petrol or diesel engine. Fuel (except electricity) for private motoring is assessed using the same percentage that applies to the car, but multiplied by a fixed amount. Pool cars are not assessable, but the conditions to qualify are stringent.

- Cheap or interest-free loans of over £10,000 are assessable on the difference between the 'official' interest rate and the interest charged. Living accommodation may be non-assessable, but otherwise is based on the annual value of the property, plus a supplementary charge for 'expensive' properties owned by the employer. Other assets provided for employees' private use are generally charged at 20% of their value. There are also some specific tax-free benefits.

- Allowable deductions are generally expenditure that is incurred wholly, exclusively and necessarily in the performance of the duties of the employment. There are also examples of certain expenditure that is allowable, including mileage payments at specified rates, professional fees and subscriptions, and pension contributions. Employees can also make tax-free donations to charities via a 'payroll giving scheme' operated by their employer.

- National Insurance Contributions are paid by employees on their cash earnings above the Primary Threshold, and by employers on cash earnings and benefits in kind.

Key terms

Pay As You Earn (PAYE) — the system that employers must operate whereby Income Tax is deducted at source from payments made to employees

benefits in kind — any reward from employment that an employee receives that is not in the form of money

company car — a car owned (or leased) by the employer that is normally available for both business and private use by an employee

pool car — a non-assessable car that is available for primarily business use by a range of employees, and is not kept at any employee's home

beneficial loan — a loan that is at a low interest rate, or is interest-free, granted to an employee by an employer

allowable deductions — expenditure that the employee has incurred that can be deducted in the calculation of the employment income assessable amount

payroll giving scheme — a scheme whereby employees can make tax-free donations to charity through their employer's payroll system

National Insurance Contributions (NICs) — a form of taxation payable by (among others) employees and employers

primary NICs — NICs payable by employees

secondary NICs — NICs payable by employers

class 1 NICs — the class of NIC relating to employment earnings

class 1A NICs — employers' NIC relating to benefits in kind

category A employees — the category that includes most working age employees

Activities

4.1 James is employed as a salesman. He receives a basic salary of £18,000 per year, plus commission that is paid on a quarterly basis in arrears.

During the period 1/1/2024 to 30/6/2025 he earned the following commissions, and received the amounts on the dates shown.

Period Commission Earned	Amount	Date Received
Jan - March 2024	£1,200	30/4/24
April - June 2024	£1,450	31/7/24
July - Sept 2024	£1,080	31/10/24
Oct - Dec 2024	£1,250	31/1/25
Jan - March 2025	£1,390	30/4/25
April - June 2025	£1,710	31/7/25

Required:

Calculate the assessable amount of employment income for 2024/25.

4.2 Analyse the following list of benefits in kind into those that are assessable, and those that are tax-free.

(a) Free meals in a staff canteen available to all staff

(b) Use of a company car (including private use)

(c) Free use of a company flat by the company accountant

(d) A £16,000 loan provided by the employer at 8% p.a. interest

(e) Free annual health screening

(f) A £2,000 computer available to take home and use privately

(g) Mileage payments at a rate of 40p per mile for using own car to drive from home to a permanent workplace

(h) Use of a 'zero-emission' van for business and private use

4.3 Julie Payd works as an Accounting Technician for IOU Limited. She was employed throughout the year at a basic salary of £20,000 per year, plus various benefits as follows.

She was provided with a company car and free private fuel throughout the tax year. The car had a petrol engine with an emission rating of 120 grams per km, and a list price of £11,500.

She had use of a company credit card to pay for fuel for the car. The amounts charged to the card for fuel amounted to £1,100 during the year. At Christmas she also spent £100 on private goods through the credit card with her employer's agreement.

She had her private healthcare insurance premium of £730 paid by IOU Ltd.

Required:

Calculate the assessable amount of employment income for Julie for the tax year.

4.4 Sue Mee is employed as a solicitor by Contrax & Company, and is paid a gross salary of £28,000 per year. She makes a contribution of 6% of her salary to an approved company pension scheme. Contrax & Company also pays a contribution into the pension fund of 7% of Sue's salary.

As a bonus, she was given vouchers to spend in a particular department store. The retail value of the vouchers was £1,000, and these cost Contrax & Company £850.

Sue is required to undertake business journeys in her own car, for which the company agreed to reimburse her at a rate of 60p per mile. She used her car for 11,500 business miles, and the company paid her the agreed amounts.

Sue pays an annual subscription to the Association of Executive Solicitors (a professional body, approved by HM Revenue & Customs). This amounted to £170. Contrax & Company did not reimburse her for this.

Sue was reimbursed £250 for hotel accommodation that she had paid for while on business trips. This was agreed as necessary business expenditure.

Required:

Calculate the employment income for Sue for the tax year.

4.5 Lettie Housego was employed by Fease & Company as an estate agent throughout the tax year. She was paid a salary of £50,000 p.a., and contributed 5% of this to the approved company pension scheme. She paid tax through PAYE of £6,000 during the tax year, although she suspects that the tax code used was incorrect.

Lettie was provided with a company car with a list price of £18,000 from the start of the tax year until 5 September. This car had a petrol engine and emission level of 187 g/km. She was not entitled to any private fuel for this car, but Fease & Company paid for business fuel.

From 6 September her car was exchanged for a new diesel car (RDE2 compliant) with a list price of £20,000 and emissions of 127 g/km. Lettie made a one-off capital contribution towards the cost of this car of £1,000. For this car Fease & Company paid for both business and private fuel.

The company pays for private dental treatment for Lettie. This cost £500.

Lettie had bought her own house through a mortgage arranged by Fease & Company. The £60,000 mortgage is on an interest only basis at a rate of 3.5% p.a.

Lettie also had dividend income of £1,000, and interest of £1,500 from a savings account with NatEast Bank.

Required:

(1) Calculate the assessable amount of employment income for Lettie for the tax year.

(2) Using an Income Tax computation for the tax year, calculate the amount of Income Tax for the year that is still owed by Lettie, or due to her.

4.6 For each statement, tick either employment or self-employment:

		Employment	Self-Employment
(a)	Contract of service is for		
(b)	Contract for services is for		
(c)	Choose work hours and charge for work done		
(d)	No need to provide own equipment		
(e)	Told how, when and where to do work		
(f)	Can employ helper or substitute		
(g)	Correct substandard work at own cost		

4.7 **(1)** On 6 September 2024, Kathy was provided with a company loan of £24,000 on which she pays interest at 1% per annum. The official rate of interest is 2.25%. On 6 January 2025 Kathy repaid £4,000.

What is the benefit in kind for 2024/25?

(2) When accommodation is purchased by an employer, what is the value of the property above which an additional benefit is applied?

(a)	£50,000	
(b)	£70,000	
(c)	£75,000	
(d)	£100,000	

(3) Would the following accommodation be treated as being job-related?

			Yes	No
(a)	Flat provided for a school caretaker			
(b)	Accommodation provided for security reasons			
(c)	Accommodation provided for all directors			

(4) Edward was provided with accommodation in the form of a flat that the employer rents. It is not job-related. The flat has an annual value of £6,800 and the employer pays a rent of £550 per month. Edward pays £100 per month towards the private use of the flat. His taxable benefit for the tax year is:

(a)	£5,600	
(b)	£6,800	
(c)	£6,600	
(d)	£5,400	

(5) Which **two** of the following statements are correct?

(a) Furniture provided by an employer is taxed at 20% per annum of the market value when first provided.

(b) Furniture provided by an employer is taxed on the cost to the employer in the year of purchase.

(c) Employees' private expenses that are paid by the employer are taxed at 20% per annum of the cost.

(d) Employees' private expenses that are paid by the employer are taxed on the cost to the employer.

4.8 An employee (who is a 40% taxpayer) has been offered a choice of one of three company cars, as follows:

- A Nissan electric car with 0% CO_2 emissions and a list price of £30,590
- A Mitsubishi plug-in hybrid petrol/electric car with emissions of 44 g/km CO_2 and a list price of £33,240. The electric-only range is 32 miles
- A Honda diesel car with emissions of 133 g/km and a list price of £30,625 which complies with RDE2

The company will provide electricity free of charge, and would also provide free fuel for the Mitsubishi or Honda. Whichever car is chosen, both the car and fuel would be available for both business and private mileage.

Complete the following table showing the total cost to the employee of each car during 2024/25. Round to the £ below where necessary.

	Nissan	Mitsubishi	Honda
Benefit % Applicable	%	%	%
Benefit for Private Use of Car	£	£	£
Benefit for Private Use of Fuel	£	£	£
Total Assessable Benefit	£	£	£
Annual Income Tax Cost	£	£	£

4.9 Complete the table below to show the monthly Class 1 NIC amounts for the following employees:

George is a category A employee who earns £1,850 per month

Helen is a category A employee who earns £5,150 per month

Natasha is a category C employee who earns £2,100 per month

Vikram is a category A employee who earns £3,910 per month

Carry out all calculations rounded down to the penny.

	Primary Contributions £	Secondary Contributions £
George		
Helen		
Natasha		
Vikram		

5 Preparing Income Tax computations

this chapter covers...

In this chapter we review the issues already covered in this book, and bring them together to ensure that we can carry out comprehensive tax computations.

We will also examine several issues that we have not covered earlier. The first of these is the payment of gift aid to charities. These payments are made net of basic rate tax, and for higher rate taxpayers there is a further adjustment needed in the tax computation.

A similar system operates for payments to personal pension schemes, and we will also illustrate how these work.

We will then examine the tax situation for those individuals with income of £100,000 or more. This can involve a reduced (or eliminated) personal allowance as well as the 'additional' tax band for taxable income over £125,140.

The final section examines practical tax planning techniques to legally and ethically reduce tax.

A REVIEW OF ASSESSABLE INCOME

what we have covered so far

In **Chapter 1** we took an overview of assessable income, and looked in outline at how the Income Tax computation works. We saw that assessable income is divided into categories so that distinct rules can be applied to each source of income.

The analysis of income that we need to be familiar with is repeated here:

'Property Income'	Rental income from land and property.
'Trading Income'	Profits from trades and professions (the self-employed and those in partnership).
'Savings and Investment Income'	UK Interest and UK Dividends.
'Employment, Pensions and Social Security Income'	Income from employment. Income Tax is deducted from employment income under the system known as Pay As You Earn (PAYE).

In **Chapter 2** we looked at income from land and property, and how it is assessed. We also saw how the assessable amount is calculated.

In **Chapter 3** we examined 'savings and investment income' in the form of savings income and dividend income. Again we saw how the basis of assessment is applied, and also learned that dividend income uses different tax rates to other income. These different rates, and the order in which income must be treated in the computation, are vital if tax is to be calculated accurately.

In **Chapter 4** we explained income from employment. This is a complex area, and we saw how benefits in kind are assessed, and what allowable deductions can be made from employment income.

The only category of income from the above list that we have not looked at in detail is 'profits from trades and professions' that is assessed as 'trading income'. We do not need to look in any detail at this type of income in this unit, since instead it forms a major part of the unit covered by Osborne Books' Business Tax text. We just need to include the assessable amount in an Income Tax computation where appropriate (see Chapter 1).

summary of tax rates for different sources of income

Set out below is a summary of what we have covered so far and a reminder of the type of income to decide the tax rate used for each source of income.

Assessable Income	Coverage in this book	Type of Income
Property Income	Chapter 2	general
Rental income (less allowable expenses), for the tax year, normally calculated on a cash basis.		
Trading Income	outline only	general
Profits (after deducting allowable expenses) for the tax year.		
Savings and Investment Income:	Chapter 3	
• Gross interest received in the tax year.		savings
• Dividends received in the tax year.		dividend
Employment Income		
Amounts received in the tax year from employment, plus the assessable value of any benefits, less any allowable deductions.	Chapter 4	general

At this stage it is worth reminding ourselves of the different tax rates for general, savings, and dividend income. These rates all use common bands, but we must work up through the bands, starting with general income, followed by savings income, and then dividend income.

	General Income	Savings Income	Dividend Income
Additional Rate/Dividend Additional Rate	45%	45%	39.35%
Higher Rate/Dividend Upper Rate	40%	40%	33.75%
Basic Rate/Dividend Ordinary Rate	20%	20%	8.75%

Remember that the Personal Savings Allowance and the Dividend Allowance can reduce the rates when applicable.

If you feel unsure about how the system works, now would be a good point to look again at Chapter 3, where it is explained in detail.

Later on we will be using the mechanism described there to carry out some comprehensive tax computations. Before we do that there are a few further topics regarding tax computations that we must be able to deal with.

EXPENDITURE THAT REDUCES TOTAL INCOME TAX

When we described property income and employment income we saw that some allowable expenditure can be deducted from the income within the category to arrive at the assessable amount. We are now going to look at two specific types of expenditure that reduce the total amount of Income Tax. They both use the same mechanism for obtaining the tax saving.

The specific payments that we are now going to look at (being tax allowable) are paid after tax has been taken off. This effectively reduces the cost to the individual making the payment.

gift aid payments

Gift aid is a government scheme that allows taxpayers to donate any amount to a charity and obtain tax relief at the highest rate that they pay.

The system operates by allowing the payer to deduct tax at 20% from the amount of the gift. The charity then claims the tax amount from HM Revenue & Customs.

Suppose, for example, a taxpayer makes a donation of £80 to a charity. The effect is to treat the payment as a gift of £100 from which tax at 20% (ie £20) has been deducted; the charity will be able to reclaim the £20 from HM Revenue & Customs. Such donations can be for any amount, and can be either a one-off gift or a regular payment. The taxpayer simply has to make a declaration to the charity that the donation(s) are to be considered as falling under the gift aid rules, and provide their name and address.

The tax treatment of gift aid payments in the individual's tax computation is as follows:

- unless the taxpayer pays tax at the higher rate, nothing needs to be done. The payer obtains tax relief by deducting 20% from the payment.

- where the taxpayer does pay tax at the higher rate, then in addition to the 20% tax relief obtained when making the payment, the basic rate band is increased by the **gross** amount of the gift. This gives further tax saving by moving some income from the higher rate into the basic rate.

So, for our example of a payment of £80 to a charity (gross equivalent of £100), the taxpayer's basic rate band would be increased in 2024/25 from £37,700 to £37,800. This will result in extra income being taxed at 20%, not 40%. The adjustment of the band enables the taxpayer to save a further (40% − 20%) 20% tax. In this example the extra tax saving is £20. This makes the effective cost of the donation only £60 (ie the total tax saving will be £20 + £20). If the taxpayer has very high income then he would also benefit from the 'additional' rate band starting point being increased by the gross equivalent of the gift aid payment. This would give an additional tax saving. We will look at the 45% rate in more detail later in this chapter.

Note that gift aid is a separate scheme from payroll giving that we looked at in Chapter 4, although an individual can make donations through both schemes if desired.

personal pension plan payments

All pension schemes work in the same general way from a tax point of view. Contributions to the schemes are allowed tax relief, but when the pension is drawn, the regular proceeds are treated as taxable.

We saw in Chapter 4 that payments to approved **occupational pension schemes** (organised by the employer) are usually given tax relief by deducting an employee's contributions in the calculation of their assessable employment income.

Personal pension plans (PPPs) may be set up by individuals who are employees or self-employed. The term also includes **stakeholder pensions** that were introduced as a government initiative, and are not dependent on the contributor being an employee or self-employed.

The mechanism for obtaining tax relief for PPPs is different from that used for an occupational pension scheme. Instead it is dealt with in the same way as donations under the gift aid scheme.

Contributions are made as net amounts – after 20% tax relief has been deducted from the gross amount payable. As with gift aid donations, the gross amount can be calculated by multiplying the net amount by 100/80. The basic rate tax band is increased by the gross amount of the taxpayer's contribution, and this enables higher rate taxpayers to obtain further relief. There is no other action to be taken in the tax computation.

Suppose a taxpayer, Tom, wanted to make gross contributions to a personal pension plan of £2,500 per year. He would make payments of £2,500 x 80% = £2,000 to his pension provider, who would reclaim the tax of £500, and invest £2,500 in the pension fund.

If he is a basic rate taxpayer, then that is the end of the matter – he has obtained the right amount of tax relief through making payments net. If he is a higher rate taxpayer then a further tax saving will arise through increasing his basic rate band by £2,500, ie moving £2,500 of his income into the basic rate band from the higher rate band. This extra saving would amount to £2,500 x (40% – 20%) = £500.

We will now use a Case Study to demonstrate how this mechanism works for these two types of payment – pension contributions and gift aid.

Case Study

DEE D'UCT:
EXPENDITURE THAT SAVES TAX

Dee is self-employed, with assessable profits for 2024/25 of £41,000. She also has rental income, with an agreed income of £15,000.

Dee has various investments, and these provided the following amounts in 2024/25:

Interest   £10,000

Dividends £6,000

required

1   Using an Income Tax computation, calculate the total tax liability for the tax year. Assume that Dee has made no gift aid or personal pension payments.

2   Now assume that in the tax year Dee made the following payments:

  • regular gift aid payments totalling £800 net (gross equivalent £1,000)

  • personal pension plan payments of £1,280 net (equivalent to £1,600 gross)

You are to recalculate Dee's Income Tax computation to take account of these two payments, and explain how the tax relief has been obtained.

solution

Task 1

Income Tax Computation 2024/25

	£	Tax Paid £
Property Income	15,000	–
Trading Income	41,000	–
Interest rec'd (as above)	10,000	–
Dividend income (as above)	6,000	–
Total Income	72,000	0
less Personal Allowance	12,570	
Taxable Income	59,430	

Analysis of Taxable Income:

	£
General Income (£15,000 + £41,000 – £12,570)	43,430
Savings Income	10,000
Dividend Income	6,000
	59,430

Income Tax Calculation:

General Income:

		£	£
£37,700	× 20%	7,540.00	
£5,730	× 40% (the rest of the £43,430)	2,292.00	
£43,430			9,832.00

Savings Income:

£500	× 0% (personal savings allowance)	0.00	
£9,500	× 40% (the rest of the £10,000)	3,800.00	
£10,000			3,800.00

Dividend Income:

£500	× 0% (dividend allowance)	0.00	
£5,500	× 33.75% (the rest of the £6,000)	1,856.25	
£6,000			1,856.25
Income Tax Liability			15,488.25

The way the tax is calculated for each category of income by working up through the bands is illustrated by the following chart (a format already seen in Chapter 3):

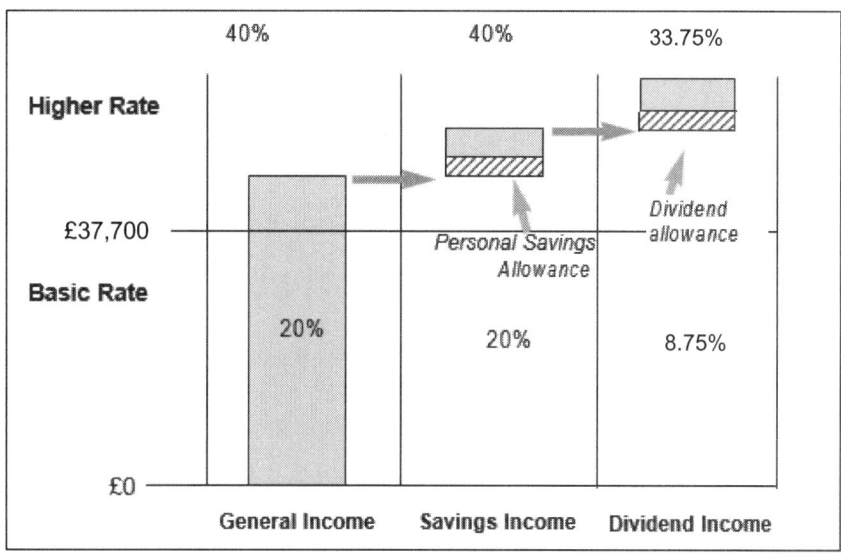

Note that in this diagram we have ignored the additional rate since it is not relevant here.

Task 2

Note firstly that the amounts payable as gift aid (£1,000) and pension plan contributions (£1,600) have only cost Dee £800 + £1,280 = £2,080.

The difference of £2,600 – £2,080 = £520 is the tax relief (20% of £2,600) that she obtained when making the payments.

The Income Tax computation in this case follows the same principles as it did in Task 1:

	£
Analysis of Taxable Income (as previously):	
General Income (£15,000 + £41,000 – £12,570)	43,430
Savings Income	10,000
Dividend Income	6,000
	59,430

Because of the payments under gift aid and to the personal pension plan, the basic rate band is now extended by (£1,000 + £1,600) from £37,700 to £40,300 cumulative.

This is used as follows:

Income Tax Calculation:

General Income:		£	£
£40,300	× 20%	8,060.00	
£3,130	× 40%	1,252.00	
£43,430			9,312.00
Savings Income:			
£500	× 0%	0.00	
£9,500	× 40%	3,800.00	
£10,000			3,800.00
Dividend Income:			
£500	× 0%	0.00	
£5,500	× 33.75%	1,856.25	
£6,000			1,856.25
Income Tax Liability			14,968.25

In this situation Dee now has to pay £14,968.25.

This compares with a payment of £15,488.25 in Task 1, a tax saving of £520 (20% of £2,600), which when added to the £520 tax relief given on the payments (when made) gives a total tax saving of £1,040 (£2,600 × 40%).

PERSONAL ALLOWANCES FOR INDIVIDUALS WITH HIGH INCOMES

When an individual has income over £100,000 the personal allowance can be restricted or eliminated entirely. This works by first calculating the individual's 'adjusted net income'.

The adjusted net income that is used to compare with the £100,000 limit is calculated as follows:

Total income from all sources*	£xx
less any grossed up gift aid payments	£(xx)
less any grossed up personal pension payments	£(xx)
'Adjusted Net Income'	£xx

*The total income from all sources is before deducting the personal allowance, personal savings allowance or dividend allowance.

If the taxpayer's adjusted net income exceeds the £100,000 limit, then the personal allowance is reduced by 50% of the difference. This means that an individual with adjusted net income of £125,140 or more would not be entitled to any personal allowance at all.

example

Jim has employment income of £95,000, plus dividends received of £15,000. He pays £2,000 per year (net) to charities under gift-aid.

Jim's adjusted net income would be:

£95,000 + £15,000 − (£2,000 x 100/80) = £107,500

This exceeds the £100,000 limit by £7,500, so Jim's personal allowance will be reduced by 50% x £7,500 = £3,750. His personal allowance will therefore be £12,570 − £3,750 = £8,820

If Jim's income had been £125,140 or more, then 50% of the excess over £100,000 would eliminate the personal allowance entirely. Note however that the allowance cannot be less than zero. There cannot be a negative personal allowance. Note that £125,140 is also the amount at which the additional rate band commences.

TAX RATES FOR INDIVIDUALS WITH HIGH INCOMES

We noted in earlier chapters that there is an 'additional rate' band that impacts on individuals who have taxable income of over £125,140. The rates that apply are 45% for general and savings income, and 39.35% for dividend income.

An individual with taxable income of over £125,140 will suffer the elimination of the personal allowance as explained in the last section. They will not be entitled to any personal savings allowance, but they will be entitled to a dividend allowance of up to £500. Although there is an extra tax band to use in the computation, the calculation follows the same principle that we have used throughout our studies. We must analyse the income into general, savings and dividend income, and then work our way up through the bands, applying the appropriate rates.

Case Study

HIGH INCOME COMPUTATION

Julie has the following income in the tax year:

	£
Trading income	120,000
Interest received	20,000
Dividends received	30,000

Her Income Tax computation for 2024/25 would appear as follows:

	£	Tax Paid £
Trading Income	120,000	
Interest	20,000	–
Dividends	30,000	–
Total Income	170,000	–
less Personal Allowance	0	
Taxable Income	170,000	

The taxable income is easily analysed since there is no personal allowance:

	£
General	120,000
Savings	20,000
Dividends	30,000

Working up through the bands:

General Income:

			£	£
£37,700	× 20%		7,540.00	
£82,300	× 40%		32,920.00	
£120,000				40,460.00

Savings Income:

			£	£
£5,140	× 40%		2,056.00	
£14,860	× 45%		6,687.00	
£20,000				8,743.00

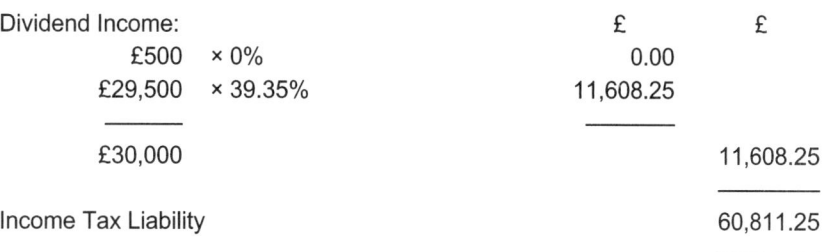

Dividend Income:		£	£
£500	× 0%	0.00	
£29,500	× 39.35%	11,608.25	
£30,000			11,608.25
Income Tax Liability			60,811.25

Note that this individual is not entitled to a personal savings allowance since she is an additional rate taxpayer.

The following diagram (which is not to scale) illustrates the calculation:

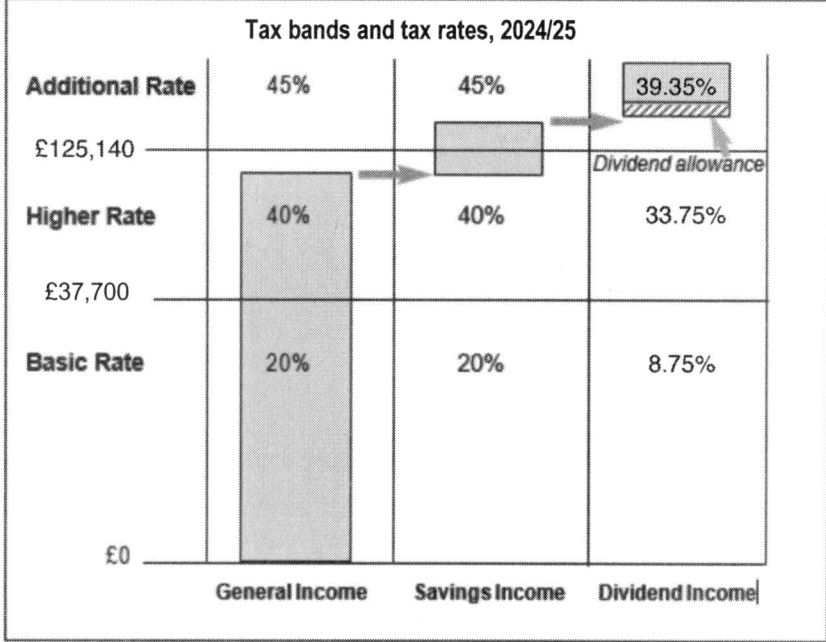

Where an individual makes gift aid and/or personal pension contributions, both the band limits of £37,700 and £125,140 are increased by the gross equivalent of the payments, and the taxpayer will therefore get increased tax relief on the payments.

> **example**
>
> If a taxpayer with an income of £165,000 (all general income) made gift aid payments of £8,000, the band limits would both be increased by £8,000 x 100/80 = £10,000. This would mean that the basic rate band would extend to £47,700, and the higher rate band would reach £135,140. In this situation the individual would pay tax as follows:
>
> | | | £ |
> |---|---|---|
> | £47,700 × 20% | | 9,540 |
> | £87,440 × 40% | | 34,976 |
> | £29,860 × 45% | | 13,437 |
> | £165,000 | | 57,953 |

DETERMINING AMOUNT OF PERSONAL SAVINGS ALLOWANCE

We have noted that the maximum personal savings allowance is reduced to £500 for higher rate taxpayers and eliminated entirely for additional rate taxpayers (as in the last Case Study).

It is often easy to see the highest band that an individual's income will fall into. However, there are some situations where it may not appear to be obvious. In these cases the 'adjusted net income' should be used to determine the band. This is the same adjusted net income that we used earlier to calculate any restriction of the personal allowance.

When the adjusted net income, less the personal allowance, is at or below £37,700, the individual will be a basic rate taxpayer, and entitled to the personal savings allowance of up to £1,000.

Where the adjusted net income, less the personal allowance, is from £37,701 to £125,140 then the individual is a higher rate taxpayer and will be entitled to up to £500 personal savings allowance.

Where the adjusted net income is over £125,140, there will be no personal savings allowance available.

> **example**
>
> Kevin has employment income of £42,300, rental income of £3,000, savings income of £1,800 and dividend income of £4,000. He pays personal pension contributions of £800 (net).
>
> The adjusted net income can be calculated as follows:

	£
Total income (£42,300 + £3,000 + £1,800 + £4,000)	51,100
less grossed up personal pension contributions	(1,000)
Adjusted net income	50,100

The adjusted net income, less the personal allowance of £12,570, equals £37,530. Since this is less than £37,700, Kevin is a basic rate taxpayer, and entitled to the personal savings allowance of £1,000.

COMPREHENSIVE TAX COMPUTATIONS

We have now examined all the issues that we need to understand to produce comprehensive Income Tax computations. All the topics covered in the following Case Study have been looked at already in this book, and it should therefore provide a good way of starting revision.

Case Study

MAX CASE:
COMPREHENSIVE TAX COMPUTATION

Max received rent from furnished property in the tax year of £11,800. He paid out allowable expenses of £1,500 in relation to the property. He has £750 of losses from property income carried forward from the previous tax year.

Max is employed as a senior manager, at a basic gross salary of £84,000 per year. Out of this his employer deducts £100 per month contribution to an approved pension scheme. Max paid £28,000 under PAYE.

He is also provided with a petrol engine company car. It had a list price of £15,600 when new, and has an emission rating of 215 grams of carbon dioxide per kilometre. Max is entitled to fuel for the car paid for by his employer for business and private motoring. Max pays an annual subscription of £130 to the Association of Company Administrators (an approved professional body).

Max has various investments, and during the tax year he received £1,000 dividends from UK companies, plus £1,400 interest from his bank accounts.

Max made a £400 donation to charity under the gift aid scheme during the tax year.

required

1   Calculate the assessable property income.

2   Calculate the assessable employment income.

3   Calculate the personal allowance for Max.

4 Using an Income Tax computation, calculate the total tax liability for the tax year, and the amount that has yet to be paid.

5 Calculate the employee's and employer's Class 1 NIC per month, assuming that Max is paid monthly.

solution

We will deal with each task in turn, selecting the appropriate data. In this Case Study the information is provided in the same order as the tasks to make the process clearer.

Task 1

	£
Property Income	
Rental received	11,800
less allowable expenditure	1,500
	10,300
less loss brought forward	750
Assessable amount	9,550

Task 2

	£
Employment Income	
Basic salary	84,000
less pension contribution	1,200
Salary per P60	82,800
add benefits:	
Company car (£15,600 × 37%)	5,772
Company car fuel (£27,800 × 37%)	10,286
	98,858
less allowable expenses (professional fees)	130
Assessable amount	98,728

Task 3

	£
Total Income:	
Property Income	9,550
Employment Income	98,728
Savings Income	1,400
Dividend Income	1,000
	110,678
less grossed-up gift aid payment	500
'Adjusted Net Income'	110,178

This exceeds the £100,000 limit by £10,178. The personal allowance is therefore reduced by 50% of this excess:

	£
Basic personal allowance	12,570
less 50% x £10,178	5,089
Revised personal allowance	7,481

Task 4

Income Tax Computation 2024/25

	£	£ Tax paid
Property Income	9,550	–
Employment Income	98,728	28,000
Savings and Investment Income:		
(interest rec'd)	1,400	–
(dividend income)	1,000	–
Total Income	110,678	28,000
Less Personal Allowance	7,481	
Taxable Income	103,197	
Analysis of Taxable Income:		
General Income (£9,550 + £98,728 – £7,481)		100,797
Savings Income		1,400
Dividend Income		1,000
		103,197

The basic rate band will be increased by the gross equivalent of the gift aid payment (£400 x 100/80 = £500).

This makes the new top of the band £37,700 + £500 = £38,200.

The income level does not reach the additional rate band.

Income Tax Calculation:

	£	£
General Income:		
£38,200 x 20%	7,640.00	
£62,597 x 40% (the rest of the £100,797)	25,038.80	
		32,678.80
Savings Income:		
£500 x 0% (personal savings allowance)	0.00	
£900 x 40% (the rest of the £1,400)	360.00	
		360.00
Dividend Income:		
£500 x 0% (dividend allowance)	0.00	
£500 x 33.75% (the rest of the £1,000)	168.75	168.75
Income Tax liability		33,207.55
less paid		28,000.00
Balance to pay		5,207.55

Task 5

Monthly pay £84,000 / 12 = £7,000

(ignore pension deduction for NIC calculations)

Employee primary Class 1 contributions:

((£4,189 – £1,048) x 8%) + ((£7,000 – £4,189) x 2%) = £307.50 per month

Employer secondary Class 1 contributions:

(£7,000 – £758) x 13.8% = £861.39 per month

TAX PLANNING TECHNIQUES

We saw in Chapter 1 that tax planning can be carried out to legally and ethically minimise tax liabilities. This involves using tax legislation in the way that it was originally intended. We will now consider practical examples of how tax planning can be carried out in connection with Income Tax. Throughout this section we must remember that tax is only one element of any financial decision – it is not worth saving tax if the decision means that other costs are increased or income reduced by more than the tax saved.

We will now consider examples based on the forms of income that we have considered in our studies.

property income

We saw in Chapter 2 that property income is normally based on profits from rentals calculated on a cash (receipts and payments) basis. Although all allowable expenditure will normally reduce profits at some point, this does provide some opportunity for bringing forward or delaying payments slightly. When carried out around the start or end of the tax year, this could be useful.

One example of a situation where care should be taken is where the property allowance of £1,000 is claimed because actual expenditure in the tax year is minimal. Additional expenditure in the year would get no tax relief if total expenditure was still below £1,000.

There may also be scope to plan the **timing** of **replacement** of assets like kitchen appliances or carpets to the taxpayer's advantage.

For example, costs incurred in the replacement of qualifying assets in March would reduce the tax liability a year earlier than if incurred a month later.

Another consideration may be the tax band that the individual was in, and how close they were to a band limit. If the individual was normally a basic rate taxpayer, but in a particular tax year was likely to become a higher rate taxpayer, it may be a good time to replace qualifying assets to reduce the income below the band limit.

savings and dividend income

There are opportunities to invest in exempt income like ISAs, since the income will be tax-free without using up the personal savings allowance. The amount to be invested each tax year is limited, but once invested, the income will remain tax-free, subject to any future changes in legislation.

Since savings and dividend income are based on the date that the income is received, there is some scope for investing in accounts that make payments at times that are most beneficial. While some accounts pay monthly interest, others pay annually on the anniversary of the account opening. Carefully selecting an appropriate account may mean that the personal savings allowance can be utilised each year.

The issue of tax bands is important for savings income, both for the tax rates themselves, and for the maximum personal savings allowance. If income can be managed so that the individual does not move up into the higher (or additional) rate, then the personal savings allowance can be most beneficial.

If the personal savings allowance and the dividend allowance can be utilised to the maximum extent, then this will clearly be a useful aid to minimising tax liability.

employment income

While renegotiating the terms of an employment contract is not a possibility for everyone, there may be situations where employees are provided with options – particularly regarding benefits in kind.

One major example would be where a company car is provided, but there is a choice of model. There are a wide variety of models with different CO_2 emissions which translate into different assessable benefits, even for cars with similar list prices.

To take an extreme example, suppose a higher rate taxpayer had the choice of a diesel car with emissions of 185 g/km or an electric car with zero CO_2 emissions, both costing £35,000. If we also assume that diesel or electricity was also provided free, the assessable benefits would work out as follows:

- diesel car (37% x £35,000) + (37% x £27,800)   = £23,236
- electric car (2% x £35,000) + 0   = £700

The difference in assessable benefit would give a tax saving of £9,014 (£22,536 x 40%) over the tax year for the electric car compared to the diesel car!

While this example gives spectacular differences (and electric cars do not suit all situations) there are tax savings to be made by carefully selecting a company car.

Another issue to be considered regarding company cars is that the assessable benefit of private fuel is the same regardless of the actual cost. Where the use of private fuel is low or moderate, it may be cheaper for the employee to pay for their own fuel than pay the tax on the benefit of free fuel.

The availability of exempt benefits is another area that may be utilised if the employer agrees. For example, interest-free loans that total £10,000 or less are tax free. Employer contributions into pension schemes are also exempt from tax.

One way that some employers and employees can save tax (and sometimes NIC) is to enter into **'salary sacrifice'** arrangements with employees. This involves an alteration to the contract of employment so that the employee receives less pay in exchange for the provision of an agreed (often tax-exempt) benefit.

Salary sacrifice schemes are widely used in some industries for a range of benefits. The Government is legislating to restrict the use of such schemes.

marginal tax rates

For any tax minimisation plan to be wholly effective it is important to be aware of the marginal rate of tax of the individual concerned. This is the highest tax rate that they pay, and is usually the rate at which tax will be saved first. For example, saving tax on general or savings income for a higher rate taxpayer will be at 40% of the income, compared with only 20% for a basic rate taxpayer.

If an individual can avoid moving into the next tax band, that will sometimes make the greatest saving. The impact of the different maximum amounts of personal savings allowance has already been noted, and this can add further importance to avoiding moving into higher bands.

For those with income just above the £100,000 level, the restriction on the personal allowance should also be considered when tax planning, since this effectively increases the marginal tax rate to 60%. Reducing adjusted net income by £1,000 would reduce tax by £600.

We saw earlier in this chapter that personal pension payments and gift-aid payments will provide tax relief at the marginal tax rate. Such payments will often provide effective ways of reducing tax liabilities.

married couples and civil partners

Where one spouse or civil partner has a different marginal tax rate to the other, then there is scope for the couple to save tax, particularly on savings or investments. There are no tax implications under Capital Gains Tax or Inheritance Tax when assets (including money or shares) are transferred between these individuals. Therefore, if it was arranged that the person with the lower rate of tax owned money in a savings account or company shares, the income generated would attract less tax for the couple. The personal savings allowance and dividend allowance should also be taken account of when sharing assets.

Where the ownership of assets in a marriage or civil partnership is being considered, tax is not the only issue, and transfer of assets should only be contemplated when the full implications are understood by both parties. Where assets are held in joint names the income arising will be split equally.

Chapter Summary

- The Income Tax computation is used to bring together income from various sources and calculate the tax. We have studied in some detail income from property and income from savings investments, together with income from employment. We only need to have an outline understanding of profits from self-employment or partnership (trading income).

- Income Tax is calculated by working up through the bands, looking at general income, followed by savings income, and finally dividend income. Each of these classifications of income use their own tax rates.

- Payments to charities under the gift aid scheme, and to pension providers for personal pension plan contributions, are made net, which provides tax relief at basic rate. Further tax relief is provided for higher and additional rate taxpayers by increasing the basic rate tax band by the gross amounts of these types of payment.

- Individuals with income over £100,000 are subject to the restriction or elimination of their personal allowance.

- Tax planning can be used ethically to minimise tax by careful timing of some transactions, use of allowances and tax-free income, and selections of benefits in kind. The individual's marginal tax rate can be used to inform relevant decisions.

Key terms

Gift Aid — a scheme whereby individuals can make payment(s) to charities as net amounts, and the charity can claim the Income Tax back; higher rate taxpayers get further relief through their tax computations

personal pension plan — a type of pension plan (including a stakeholder pension) arranged for an individual – basic rate tax relief is provided by making payments net of 20% Income Tax while higher rate and additional rate taxpayers get further relief through their tax computations

salary sacrifice scheme — the alteration to the contract of employment so that the employee receives less pay in exchange for the provision of an agreed (often tax exempt) benefit

Activities

5.1 Jo paid £2,000 (net) under the gift aid scheme and £3,040 (net) to her pension provider as personal pension plan contributions. Her total taxable pay is £50,000 (all general income) after deducting her personal allowance.

Calculate:

(a) The gross equivalent of each payment.

(b) The effective cost to her of each payment, after taking into account higher rate tax relief.

5.2 Matt has the following assessable income for the tax year:

Rental Income	£9,400
Employment Income	£30,000 (tax paid under PAYE £3,486)
Gross Interest Received	£5,000
Dividends	£12,000

He paid £2,400 (net) to a personal pension plan during the tax year.

Required:

Using an Income Tax computation, calculate the Income Tax liability and the amount of tax that is outstanding.

5.3 John has the following income in the tax year:

- Employment income £46,145
- Interest from ISAs £1,020
- Bank account interest £630
- Dividends £3,500

John paid £300 (net) under gift aid.

Calculate John's adjusted net income and state the amount of personal savings allowance that he will be entitled to.

5.4 Mike received rent from furnished property in the tax year of £6,300. He paid out insurance of £350 in relation to the property, and spent £700 replacing a carpet. He has £250 of losses against property income carried forward from the previous year.

Mike is employed as an accountant, at a gross salary of £148,525 per year. He paid £53,000 under PAYE.

Mike uses his own car for occasional company business trips. During the tax year he travelled 2,000 business miles, and was reimbursed by his employer at 80p per mile. Mike paid his membership fees of £283 to the ACCA.

Mike has various investments, and during the tax year he received £1,400 in dividends from UK companies, plus £1,000 interest from his bank accounts.

Required:

(a) Calculate the assessable property income.

(b) Calculate the assessable employment income.

(c) Using an Income Tax computation, calculate the total tax liability for the tax year, and the amount that has yet to be paid.

5.5 During the tax year, Rachel had employment income of £110,000 and received dividends of £6,000.

Required:

Calculate her total Income Tax liability (ie before deduction of tax paid) for the tax year, using the table given below. Round amounts to £ below.

	£
Employment income	
Dividends	
Personal allowance	
Taxable income	

5.6 Jim is a higher rate taxpayer with savings income in excess of the personal savings allowance. From the following list of separate possible actions, select those that will reduce his total Income Tax liability. You do not need to consider what impact the actions have on Jim's overall financial position.

Action		Select
(a)	Withdraw savings from bank account and invest them in cash ISA	
(b)	Change company car from petrol model of same registered date to diesel model with same list price and same CO_2 emissions of 100 g/km	
(c)	Make payments into personal pension plan	
(d)	Borrow £8,000 interest-free from employer and use proceeds to pay off personal credit card	
(e)	Spend £1,000 replacing carpets in house that he rents to a tenant and generates profits of £3,000 per year after £2,000 expenses	
(f)	Donate money to charity through payroll giving scheme	

5.7 During the tax year, Robert had employment income of £109,000 and received dividends of £5,000. He paid £2,400 (net) into a personal pension scheme.

Calculate his total Income Tax liability (ie before deduction of tax paid), using the table given below. Round amounts to £ below.

	£
Employment income	
Dividends	
Personal allowance	
Taxable income	

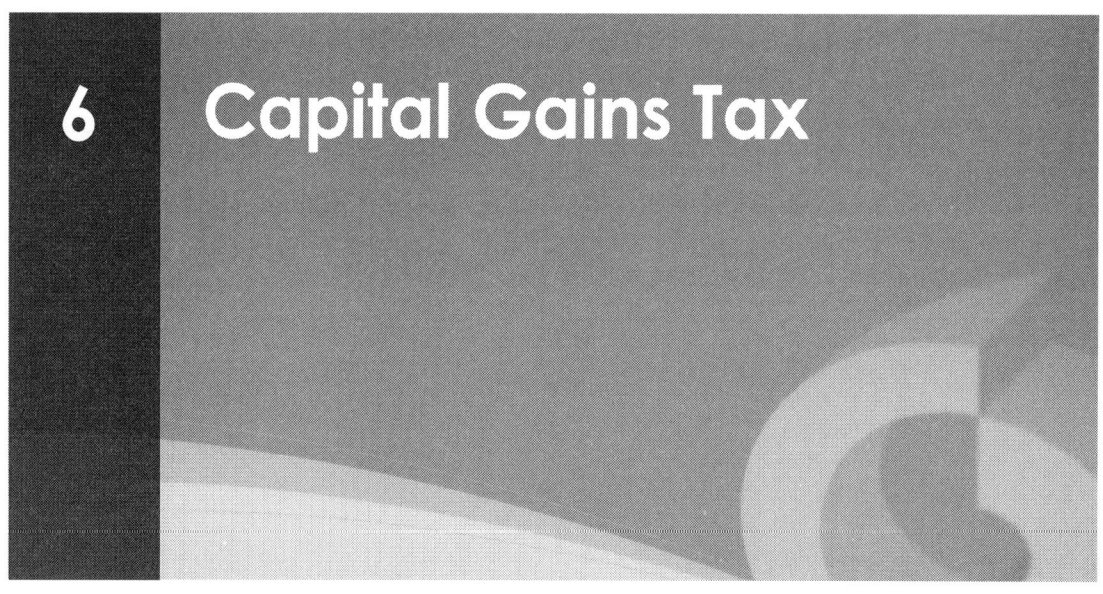

6 Capital Gains Tax

this chapter covers...

In this chapter we examine Capital Gains Tax (CGT). This is a tax on the gains made on disposal of capital assets, and we will define a disposal, before examining which assets are chargeable and which are exempt.

We will then see how Capital Gains Tax is calculated, by using the annual exemption and the appropriate rate of tax.

Next we look in detail at the calculations of each gain or loss, including the special rules that apply to spouses, civil partners and connected persons. In this section we learn what expenses can form allowable deductions in our calculations.

Losses and how they are relieved are examined next, and we will see how they are first set against the gains of the same tax year, before being carried forward if necessary.

We then learn how to calculate gains or losses when only part of an asset has been disposed of and the remaining part is kept. We use cost apportionment based on valuations at the date of sale to do this.

We then see how capital improvement (or 'enhancement') expenditure can form an allowable cost in the gains computation.

Next we examine the rather complicated rules surrounding private residence relief that apply when a property is not occupied throughout its ownership.

The final section deals with shares and the special rules relating to matching, pooling, and bonus and rights issues.

AN INTRODUCTION TO CAPITAL GAINS TAX

Capital Gains Tax (CGT) applies in certain circumstances to individuals who dispose of capital assets that they have previously acquired. It often applies to the sale or gift of an asset that may have been owned for quite some time. This can result in what is called a 'chargeable gain'. Note that CGT does not apply to trading assets, where items are regularly bought and sold to make a profit, as these are not classed as capital assets.

Although Capital Gains Tax applies to both personal assets and business assets, we are only going to examine how it applies to personal assets in this book. Gains on the disposal of business assets are dealt with in the unit 'Business Tax' (see Osborne Books' Business Tax Tutorial and Workbook).

basis of assessment

Capital Gains Tax is applied to individuals by using the same tax years as those used for Income Tax. The basis of assessment for Capital Gains Tax is the **chargeable gains less capital losses** arising from disposals that occur during the tax year.

We will look at how losses are dealt with later in this chapter. The main issues to understand at this point are that the tax is based on the total (or aggregate) of gains that have occurred, and that a gain can only arise when a disposal has taken place.

disposals

A disposal arises when an asset is:

- sold (or part of it is sold)
- given away
- lost, or
- destroyed

Most of the situations that we will come across will be based on the sale or gift of an asset. You should remember, however, that a disposal can also result from loss or destruction of an asset. In the case of loss and destruction, the value of the asset is most likely to be assessed as zero, unless insurance proceeds are received.

Two special situations where disposals do not give rise to Capital Gains Tax are:

- disposals arising because the owner has died, and
- any disposal between spouses (husband and wife) or civil partners

CHARGEABLE AND EXEMPT ASSETS

For Capital Gains Tax to arise, the asset that has been disposed of must be a 'chargeable' asset. Exempt assets are entirely outside of the CGT system. Instead of there being a long list of the assets that are chargeable, there is a fairly short list of assets that are exempt.

The simple rule is that if an asset is not exempt, then it must be chargeable!

A list of the main exempt assets is set out below:

exempt assets

- private residence – an individual's only or main home (we will look at the rules for this later)
- cars
- wasting chattels (chattels are tangible, movable items; wasting means they have an estimated life of less than 50 years). Items of machinery for personal use (including, for example, clocks) are normally considered wasting chattels
- chattels bought and sold for £6,000 or less (there are also some special rules for those sold for more than £6,000 that we will look at later)
- government securities (gilts)
- gifts made to charity
- shares that are held in an ISA

chargeable assets

Some typical personal assets that are chargeable and regularly feature in examination tasks include:

- antique furniture and paintings (since they have already lasted over 50 years)
- holiday homes
- land (eg a field not part of a main residence)
- shares

You must remember that these are only examples – all assets are chargeable unless they are exempt.

CALCULATION OF CAPITAL GAINS TAX

All individuals are entitled to an annual exempt amount – an **annual exemption** – for each tax year. This works in a similar way to a personal allowance under Income Tax. The exempt amount is deducted from the total net gains that have been calculated on the individual assets that have been disposed of during the year. Capital Gains Tax is then worked out on the balance.

The exempt amount is £3,000 in 2024/25. The exempt amount can only be used against capital gains (not set against income), and cannot be carried back or forward and used in another tax year.

Once the exempt amount has been deducted from the total net gains, the balance is subject to Capital Gains Tax. The rates of Capital Gains Tax are 10% and 20% for gains on all assets with the exception of those relating to disposals of residential property.

Although Capital Gains Tax is a separate tax from Income Tax, it uses the same band structure. Gains are treated as if they were added on top of taxable income, and the 10% rate is applied to gains falling within the basic rate band while the 20% rate applies to gains within the higher or additional rate bands.

The following diagram (which is an extended version of the one used earlier to illustrate Income Tax bands, and is not to scale) shows how the system works.

	Tax bands and tax rates, 2024/25			
Additional Rate £125,400	45%	45%	39.35%	
Higher Rate	40%	40%	33.75%	20%
£37,700				
Basic Rate	20%	20%	8.75%	10%
£0				
	General Income	Savings	Dividends	Capital Gains Tax
	←	Income Tax	→	

If an individual is already a higher rate or additional rate taxpayer then any gains will be taxed at 20%. Where the taxpayer pays Income Tax only at the basic rate then gains will be taxed at 10% provided they do not exceed the basic rate band of £37,700 when added to taxable income. Where they do exceed this amount the excess will be taxed at 20%. The following example will illustrate the situation.

> **example**
>
> Rashid has total taxable general income of £30,200 after deducting his personal allowance. He made capital gains of £15,700 before deducting his exempt amount. The gains do not relate to residential property.
>
> Rashid has taxable gains of £15,700 – £3,000 (exempt amount) = £12,700. He has £37,700 – £30,200 = £7,500 remaining in his basic rate band after accounting for his taxable income. Therefore £7,500 of his gains will be taxed at 10%, and the remainder taxed at 20%, as follows:
>
> | | |
> |---|---:|
> | £7,500 x 10% | £750.00 |
> | £5,200 (the remainder of the £12,700) x 20% | £1,040.00 |
> | Total Capital Gains Tax | £1,790.00 |

We must now turn our attention to how to calculate the chargeable gain or loss on each separate disposal.

THE COMPUTATION OF EACH GAIN

Each disposal of a chargeable asset requires a calculation to determine the amount of any gain or loss. This computation follows a standard format that is in effect a mini income statement (profit & loss account) for the item disposed of. There are some minor variations to this format in particular circumstances, as we will see later. The basic format is as follows:

	£
Proceeds on disposal	X
less	
Incidental costs of disposal	(X)
Net proceeds	X
less	
Original cost	(X)
Incidental costs of acquisition	(X)
Gain (or loss)	X

proceeds on disposal

This normally refers to the amount that the asset realised when it was disposed of – ie the selling price. However, there are some special situations where the figure used is different:

- if the asset was given away (to anyone), or sold to a 'connected' person at less than the market value, the **market value** is used in the computation instead of the actual amount received. A chargeable gain can therefore arise even though the person disposing of the asset has received no proceeds

- if the asset has been lost or destroyed then the asset will have been disposed of for zero proceeds, and zero will be used in the computation – and there could be a loss. The exception to this would be if an insurance claim has been made, in which case the amount of the claim proceeds would be used

transfer to spouse or civil partner

When an asset is transferred to a spouse or civil partner, no capital gain arises, as mentioned earlier. This is achieved by treating the disposal proceeds as the amount needed to generate exactly zero gain or loss.

For example, if a wife had bought an asset some time ago for £10,000 (with no other costs) and gave it to her husband, the disposal proceeds would be treated as £10,000 so that no gain would arise. This would also mean that if the husband later sold the asset, his cost would also be considered to be £10,000, and any gain calculated on that basis.

A transfer between spouses or civil partners is often known as being made on a 'no gain, no loss' basis.

transfer to 'connected person'

As already noted, when an asset is sold to a connected person at less than market value, the market value is used in the computation of gains.

The following relatives of the person disposing of the asset are 'connected persons', and so are the relatives' spouses or civil partners:

- ancestors and spouse's ancestors (parent, grandparent, etc)
- siblings and spouse's siblings (brother, sister)
- lineal descendants and spouse's lineal descendants (child, grandchild, etc)

So, for example, the following people **would** each be a **connected person**, and any disposal would be deemed to be at market value:

- brother's wife
- wife's grandfather
- daughter's husband

Each of the following people (for example) **would not** be a **connected person**:

- uncle or aunt
- cousin
- friend

Remember that gifts (whether to a connected person or not) are always deemed to be a disposal at market value, unless they are to a spouse or civil partner.

If a loss is incurred on a disposal to a connected person, the loss cannot be set against general gains, but can only be set against gains made on other disposals to the same person.

incidental costs of disposal

Incidental costs are the costs incurred by the taxpayer in selling the asset. Examples include advertising expenses, auction costs, or estate agent's fees for selling a property.

original cost, and incidental costs of acquisition

This relates to the amount paid to acquire the asset in the first place, plus any other costs incurred to buy it. Examples of these costs would include legal fees or auction costs. If the asset was given or bequeathed to the taxpayer, the market value at that time is used. We will examine shortly how to deal with expenditure incurred later to improve the asset.

Case Study

HOLLY DAY: COMPUTATION OF GAIN

Holly bought a field in Cornwall in August 1990 as an investment. She paid £59,000 for the field, and also paid legal fees of £1,000 at the same time to arrange the purchase.

In the current tax year Holly sold the field for £240,000. The estate agent's fees for the sale were £3,000, and she incurred further legal fees of £2,000.

The field was Holly's only disposal of a chargeable asset during the tax year.

Holly is a higher rate Income Tax payer.

required

Calculate the gain on the disposal of the field, and the amount of Capital Gains Tax that Holly must pay.

solution

	£
Proceeds on disposal	240,000
less Incidental costs of disposal	(5,000)
Net proceeds	235,000
less	
Original cost	(59,000)
Incidental costs of acquisition	(1,000)
Gain	175,000

	£
Total gains for the tax year	175,000
less exempt amount	(3,000)
Subject to CGT	172,000

Capital Gains Tax
£172,000 x 20% = £34,400

Holly pays CGT at 20% because she is already a higher rate taxpayer under Income Tax.

DEALING WITH LOSSES

Capital losses arise from disposals in the same way as gains.

When losses have been calculated they are dealt with as follows:

- they are firstly set against gains arising in the same tax year, until these are reduced to zero, then
- any unused loss is carried forward to set against the next gains that arise in future tax years – at this stage the annual exempt amount can be safeguarded

We will now use an example to illustrate how this works.

example

Kulvinder has the following capital gains and losses, based on disposals occurring in the following tax years.

	2022/23 £	2023/24 £	2024/25 £
Gains	20,000	17,000	28,000
Losses	(35,000)		

The annual exempt amount was £12,300 in 2022/23. It was £6,000 in 2023/24. It is £3,000 in 2024/25.

required

Calculate how the loss can be used to offset the gains, and the amount subject to CGT each year.

2022/23

Because the loss of £35,000 occurred in the same year as the gain of £20,000, we must set off as much loss as possible against the gain, until the net gain is reduced to zero. There is no CGT liability this year. We then carry the loss balance of (£35,000 – £20,000 = £15,000) on to the next year.

2023/24

We now have a brought forward loss, and can offset it against the current gains. However, because the loss is brought forward we only need to use up enough loss to bring the net gain down to the exempt amount.

We therefore use up £11,000 of the brought forward loss – just enough to bring the net gains for this year down to the exempt amount. There is no CGT liability in this year, and a loss of (£15,000 – £11,000 = £4,000) to carry forward.

2024/25

This year the remaining loss of £4,000 that has been brought forward is set against the gain of £28,000. From the balance of £24,000 is deducted the exempt amount of £3,000, leaving £21,000 that is subject to tax.

Summary

	2022/23 £	2023/24 £	2024/25 £
Losses working			
Loss brought forward	0	15,000	4,000
Loss incurred	35,000	0	0
Loss used up	20,000	11,000	4,000
Loss carried forward	15,000	4,000	0
Calculation of gains			
Gains	20,000	17,000	28,000
Loss set off	(20,000)	(11,000)	(4,000)
Net gains	0	6,000	24,000
Less exempt amount		(6,000)	(3,000)
Amount subject to CGT	0	0	21,000

Now apply what you have learnt about capital gains so far by working through the comprehensive Case Study that follows.

Case Study

IVOR LOTT: CAPITAL GAINS TAX PRINCIPLES

Ivor Lott made the following disposals during the tax year. Ivor has taxable income of £20,000 (after deducting his personal allowance).

- He sold his entire holding of 3,000 shares that he owned in Expo Limited for £6.75 each. He had bought all the shares in August 1998 for £10.00 each.
- He sold an antique table for £15,000 that he had bought in July 1996 for £7,000.
- He gave his daughter a field that was located 3 miles away from his home. He bought the field in April 1985 for £2,000. It was valued at £150,000 at the time of the gift, since it was now a possible development site.
- He sold his Jaguar E-type car for £25,000. He had owned the car since January 1983 when he had bought it for £5,000.

required

- Calculate any gain or loss on each disposal.
- Calculate the Capital Gains Tax payable by Ivor for the tax year (to the nearest £).

solution

Shares in Expo Limited

	£
Proceeds (3,000 x £6.75)	20,250
less cost (3,000 x £10)	(30,000)
Capital loss	(9,750)

Antique table

Proceeds	15,000
less cost	(7,000)
Gain	8,000

Field

Market Value	150,000
less cost	(2,000)
Gain	148,000

A gain arises even though Ivor received no proceeds.

Car

This asset is exempt from Capital Gains Tax.

We can now add together the gains, and offset the loss.

	£
Gains:	
Antique table	8,000
Field	148,000
	156,000
less loss on shares	(9,750)
Net gains	146,250
less exempt amount	(3,000)
Subject to CGT	143,250

Capital Gains Tax

	£
£17,700* x 10%	1,770.00
£125,550 x 20%	25,110.00
£143,250	26,880.00

*£37,700 – £20,000 taxable income

DEALING WITH PART DISPOSALS

We saw earlier that a disposal for Capital Gains Tax (CGT) purposes can relate to all or part of an asset. Although part disposal will not apply to many assets that are not divisible, it could apply (for example) to a piece of land.

If an asset was acquired as a whole, and then part of it is sold while the rest is retained, we need to compute the gain (or loss) on the part that was disposed of. The difficulty is that although we know how much the proceeds are for that part of the asset, we probably don't know how much of the original cost of the whole asset relates to that portion.

The way that this issue is tackled is to value the remaining part of the asset at the time of the part disposal. The original cost can then be apportioned by using these figures.

The cost applicable to the part disposed of is:

$$\text{Original cost of whole asset} \times \frac{A}{(A + B)}$$

where A = Proceeds (or market value) of part disposed of, and
       B = Market value of part retained

The following example will illustrate the calculation.

example

Heather bought a large field for £4,000 in January 1991 to keep her horses. In the current tax year she sold a part of the field for £3,000. At the same time the remainder of the field was valued at £9,000.

The portion of the original cost relating to the part of the field that was sold would be calculated as:

$$£4,000 \times \frac{£3,000}{(£3,000 + £9,000)}$$

This gives the cost as $£4,000 \times \frac{3,000}{12,000} = £1,000$

The computation would then be carried out in the normal way:

	£
Proceeds	3,000
less cost (as calculated)	(1,000)
Gain	2,000

IMPROVEMENT EXPENDITURE

Where expenditure after acquisition is incurred to enhance an asset, and it is then disposed of in this improved condition, the improvement expenditure forms an allowable cost in the computation.

The expenditure must be of a 'capital' nature, and examples of this could include extending a building or having an antique professionally restored.

The following example illustrates the situation.

example

Sonny Daze bought an antique painting for £60,000 in September 1984. In January 1990 he spent £40,000 having the painting professionally restored. He sold the painting in the current tax year for £300,000.

		£
Proceeds		300,000
less	original cost	(60,000)
	improvement expenditure	(40,000)
Gain		200,000

PRIVATE RESIDENCES

We saw earlier in the chapter that a taxpayer's only or main residence is exempt from Capital Gains Tax through 'Private Residence Relief' (PRR). Properties that have never been used as a main residence (for example holiday homes) are fully chargeable.

Where a taxpayer has two properties, and uses them both as residences, only one can be treated as a main residence, and the taxpayer can elect as to which one it is. The election must be made to HMRC within two years of acquiring the second property. This could occur, for example, if a taxpayer used a property near his workplace during the week and another property situated elsewhere at weekends.

A property's status may change if it is occupied as a main residence for only part of its period of ownership. If this happens and the property is subsequently disposed of, a gain can arise. In these circumstances the gain is worked out initially based on the whole period of ownership, and then apportioned to arrive at the exempt gain by multiplying the total gain by:

$$\frac{\text{period of occupation (as a main residence)}}{\text{period of ownership}}$$

Provided a property has been a main residence for some time during its ownership then the last nine months of ownership are always regarded as part of the main residence occupation period. This is the case even if there is another main residence in use during that time.

We will now illustrate this using an example.

example

James bought a cottage in the Lake District for £50,000 on 1 January 1997 to use as a holiday home. He retired on 1 January 2007, and decided to sell his main home and move into the cottage. On 1 January 2012 he bought a house in the Cotswolds as his new main residence, moved there and went back to using the Lake District cottage as a holiday home.

On 1 January 2025 he sold the cottage in the Lake District for £250,000.

We first calculate the gain based on the whole period of ownership.

	£
Proceeds	250,000
less cost	(50,000)
Gain for whole period	200,000

We then time apportion the gain, counting the last nine months of ownership as occupation, regardless of whether it actually was.

Owned: 1/1/97 - 1/1/25 = 28 years = 336 months

Actually occupied as main home: 1/1/07 - 1/1/12 = 5 years = 60 months

Deemed occupation as main residence: 1/4/24 - 1/1/25 = 9 months

Total actual and deemed occupation = 69 months

Exempt gain: £200,000 x 69/336 = £41.071 (PRR)

Chargeable gain: £200,000 x 267/336 = £158,929

In addition to the above rule, there are other periods of absence that will count as being occupied as a main residence, provided:

- the property was **actually occupied** as a main residence at some time both **before** and **after** the period, and
- no other property is being treated as a main residence during the period of absence

These additional periods of 'deemed occupation' are:

- three years in total for any reason
- up to four years when the taxpayer is absent due to UK employment
- any period when the taxpayer is living abroad due to employment

Case Study

LOVELY MOVER: PRIVATE RESIDENCE

Simon Lovely bought a house in London on 1 July 1999 for £50,000. He lived in it as his main residence until 1 January 2007 when he started a new job in Scotland. He rented a flat in Edinburgh to live in, but he kept his London house. On 1 July 2016, he left his job in Scotland, and moved back into his London house. On 1 January 2018 he bought a house in Cornwall, which he elected to be his main home and moved out of his London house. On 1 July 2024, he sold his London house for £510,000.

He made no other disposals in the tax year.

required

- Calculate the chargeable gain on disposal of the London house.

solution

	£
Sale proceeds	510,000
less cost	(50,000)
Gain before PRR relief	460,000

		Ownership (Years)	Actual/deemed occupation (Years)
Actual Occupation	1/7/99 - 1/1/07	7.5	7.5
Working in UK	1/1/07 - 1/7/16	9.5	7 *(see below)
Actual Occupation	1/7/16 - 1/1/18	1.5	1.5
Absence	1/1/18 - 1/7/24	6.5	0.75 (last 9 months)
Total ownership		25	
Actual/deemed occupation			16.75

*The deemed occupation periods for 'working elsewhere in the UK' (4 years maximum) and 'absence for any reason' (3 years maximum) can both be claimed making a total of 7 years.

		£
Exempt gain	460,000 x 16.75/25 =	308,200
Chargeable gain	460,000 x 8.25/25 =	151,800

	£
Gain	151,800
Annual exemption	(3,000)
Amount subject to Capital Gains Tax	148,800

SPECIAL RULES FOR CHATTELS

Chattels are tangible, moveable items such as furniture, jewellery, works of art and vehicles. As we saw in the last chapter, certain chattels are entirely exempt from Capital Gains Tax. These exempt chattels are:

- wasting chattels (those with an expected life of less than 50 years)
- cars
- chattels that are both bought and sold for £6,000 or less

There are also some special rules about the amount of gain or loss that can occur when chargeable chattels are disposed of. Although these rules are not particularly complicated, they do need to be remembered.

chattels sold at a gain for over £6,000

In this situation the gain is limited to an amount of:

5/3 (Proceeds – £6,000)

The 'proceeds' in this calculation are the gross proceeds – the amount received before deducting any selling expenses.

This is sometimes known as the 'chattel marginal relief'. Suppose gains had been calculated on disposals as follows:

Disposal A
Proceeds	£9,000
Cost	£1,500
Gain	£7,500

The gain would be restricted to 5/3 (£9,000 – £6,000) = £5,000

£5,000 would therefore be used as the gain figure, since it is less than the £7,500 based on the normal calculation.

Disposal B
Proceeds	£9,000
Cost	£6,500
Gain	£2,500

Here the gain would also be restricted to £5,000, but since the calculated gain is only £2,500 the restriction would have no effect. The £2,500 gain would therefore stand.

chattels sold at a loss for less than £6,000

If the chattel had also been bought for less than £6,000 the transaction would be exempt from CGT. If the chattel had been acquired for over £6,000 then the loss would be limited by substituting £6,000 for the actual proceeds in the calculation.

For example, a chattel bought for £8,000 and sold for £3,000 would have a loss calculated as:

	£
Deemed proceeds	6,000
less actual cost	(8,000)
Loss	(2,000)

Make sure that you understand this process, and remember that it is the proceeds that are deemed to be £6,000. This is an area where it is easy to get confused if you are not careful.

We will now use a Case Study to help consolidate our understanding of the main issues that we have covered in this chapter so far.

JUSTIN CREASE: USING SPECIAL RULES

Case Study

Justin made the following disposals in the tax year. He is a higher rate Income Tax payer.

- He sold an antique lamp for £7,500. The lamp had cost £4,200 when he bought it in January 1999.
- He sold part of a large field for £10,000. He had bought the whole field in January 1990 for £8,000. At the time of the sale the market value of the remaining part of the field was £30,000.
- He sold a house in September 2024 for £325,000. He had bought the house in January 2007 for £160,000, and immediately used it as his main residence. He bought a new house in February 2024, and nominated that as his main residence. He rented out the original house from February 2024 until it was sold.
- He sold his gold cufflinks for £5,000. They had been left to him in his Uncle's will in September 1995. The value of the cufflinks at that time was £7,800.
- He bought an antique painting in January 1990 for £25,000. In September 1995 he paid £15,000 to have it professionally restored. The restored painting was sold for £90,000.

required

- Calculate the gain or loss on each applicable disposal.
- Calculate the amount of Capital Gains Tax that Justin will have to pay in respect of the tax year.

solution

Antique Lamp	£
Proceeds	7,500
less cost	(4,200)
Gain	3,300

but gain restricted to:
5/3 (£7,500 – £6,000) = £2,500

Field

Proceeds	10,000
less apportioned cost:	(2,000)
£8,000 x £10,000 / (£10,000 + £30,000)	
Gain	8,000

House

The house is entirely exempt. The period when it was rented out still counts as being occupied, as it is less than nine months, and occurs at the end of the ownership period.

Cufflinks

	£
Deemed proceeds	6,000
less value at acquisition	(7,800)
Loss	(1,800)

Antique painting

	£
Proceeds	90,000
less cost	(25,000)
improvement expenditure	(15,000)
Gain	50,000

We can now add together the gains, and set off the loss.

	£
Gains	
Antique Lamp	2,500
Field	8,000
Antique painting	50,000
	60,500
less loss on cufflinks	(1,800)
Net gains	58,700
less exempt amount	(3,000)
Subject to CGT	55,700

Capital Gains Tax
£55,700 x 20% = £11,140

MATCHING RULES FOR SHARES

We saw earlier that shares are chargeable assets, and that the computation for the acquisition and subsequent disposal of a block of shares is the same as for other assets.

The complication that can arise is when various quantities of the same type of share in the same company are bought and sold. The problem faced is similar to that in any stock valuation situation – how to determine which of the shares that were bought are deemed to be the same ones that were sold. The dilemma is solved in this situation by the application of strict **matching rules**.

When some shares are sold, the matching process is carried out by working down the following categories of acquisition, skipping any that do not apply, until all the shares sold have been matched. A separate CGT computation is then used for each separate match.

1 Firstly, any shares bought on the **same day** that the disposal occurs are matched with that disposal.

2 Secondly, any shares bought in the **30 days after** the disposal are matched with those disposed of (matching the earliest first if more than one acquisition). This probably seems illogical – selling something before it is bought!

3 Thirdly, any remaining shares not yet matched are deemed to have come from the 'FA 1985 pool' of shares. This is a device for merging shares.

The above order of matching is illustrated in the diagram below. The numbers in the diagram relate to the numbered stages described above.

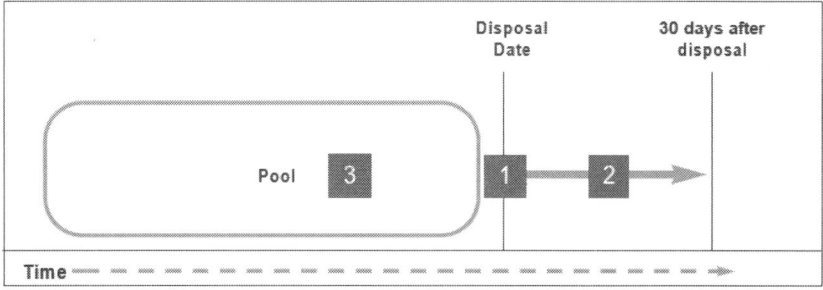

Remember that this matching process only applies where there have been several purchases of the same type of shares in the same company. It does not apply to a mixture of different companies' shares, nor is it needed where a shareholding is bought and sold intact.

USING THE 'FA 1985 POOL'

This device was introduced in the 1985 Finance Act, and merges (or 'pools') shares in the same company and of the same type together. As we just saw, it occurs as the last of the matching rules, and is used to calculate the cost of shares acquired before the disposal date.

It is similar to the calculation of weighted average inventory valuations (as you have probably studied in Costing).

The pool needs to keep data relating to:

- numbers of shares and
- actual costs

These form the two main columns of the pool working.

The pool commences with the first shares bought. It then moves forward in time, adding each subsequent purchase of shares to provide cumulative numbers and costs of shares in the pool.

When any shares from the pool are disposed of, a proportion of the cumulative cost at the time of disposal is deducted from the pool, based on the numbers of shares. This cost amount that is deducted from the pool is then used in the gains calculation and compared with the proceeds in the normal way.

We will now demonstrate how the process works using a numerical example.

example

On 1/1/2025 Julie sold 10,000 ordinary shares in WyeCo Ltd for £10 each, from her shareholding of 25,000. Her shareholding had been built up as follows:

  1/1/1988 bought 17,000 shares for £5.00 each

  1/1/1993 bought 8,000 shares for £7.00 each

Since there are no acquisitions on or after 1/1/2025, the whole of the disposal of 10,000 shares will be matched with the pool. The pool will be built up as follows, with the disposal deducted as the latest transaction:

	Number	Cost £
1/1/1988 Purchase	17,000	85,000
1/1/1993 Purchase	8,000	56,000
Pool Totals	25,000	141,000
less Disposal	(10,000)	(56,400)
Pool Balance after disposal	15,000	84,600

You should note the following:

- the cost figures for the disposal are a proportional amount of the pool costs before disposal, based on the number of shares (eg £141,000 x 10,000 / 25,000 = £56,400)

The computation for the disposal will now appear as follows:

	£
Proceeds (10,000 x £10)	100,000
less cost	(56,400)
Gain	43,600

If at some future date there was another disposal of shares from the pool then the pool balance remaining (as above) would be used to determine the cost of the shares in the further disposal.

BONUS AND RIGHTS ISSUES

dealing with bonus shares

Bonus shares are additional shares given free to shareholders based on their current shareholding. This is sometimes called a 'scrip issue' and may be carried out as part of a capital restructuring of the company.

For CGT purposes the bonus shares are treated as if they were acquired at the same time as the original shares that generated the issue. For example, a shareholder who owned 1,000 shares that were bought in January 2001 would be entitled to a further 200 shares if, later on, there were a bonus issue of 'one for five' shares. The total of 1,200 shares would be treated as bought in January 2001 for the amount paid for the 1,000 shares.

In virtually all situations, bonus shares are added to the pool when they are received. Since no payment is made, there is no adjustment to the cost figure.

If the bonus shares are received based on several acquisitions of original shares, the bonus shares will still be added into the pool, since the original shares will also be in the pool.

dealing with rights issues

A **rights issue** is the situation where additional shares are sold to existing shareholders, usually at a special price. For matching purposes, the shares that are bought in this way are treated as if they were bought with the original shares.

Rights issue shares will join the pool and be treated like any other share purchase. Their cost will be added into the pool.

We will now use a Case Study to make sure the principles relating to various matters studied are clear.

Case Study

CHER BYERS:
GAINS INCLUDING SHARES AND POOLING

Cher had acquired the following quoted ordinary shares in AbCo Plc (a listed company).

1/5/1985	1,000 shares at £4.00 each	£4,000
1/1/1990	Bonus issue of 1 for 4	
1/1/1992	1,750 shares at £4.20 each	£7,350
1/1/1995	1,500 shares at £4.10 each	£6,150 (Rights issue)
1/12/2001	1,800 shares at £5.10 each	£9,180

On 15/11/2001 she had sold 1,000 of her shareholding.

On 15/8/2024 she sold a further 2,500 ordinary shares in AbCo Plc for £10.00 each.

Cher also made the following disposals during 2024/25:

- She sold a plot of land for £20,000. This originally formed part of a larger field that she bought for £15,000 in January 1992. At the time of the sale the remaining portion of land was valued at £40,000.

- She sold an antique ring for £6,600. She had bought it on 1 January 1999 for £3,500.

- She sold an antique painting for £10,000. She had bought it in December 1996 for £14,000.

Cher has taxable income of £29,200 (after deducting her personal allowance).

required

1. Identify which shares would have already been matched against the disposal that took place on 15/11/2001.
2. Show how the disposal of shares on 15/8/2024 will be matched against the acquisitions, and
3. Calculate the total gain arising from the sale of shares that took place on 15/8/2024.
4. Calculate any gains or losses arising from the disposal of the other assets.
5. Calculate the total Capital Gains Tax payable in respect of the tax year.

solution

1. The disposal of 1,000 shares on 15/11/2001 would have been matched with 1,000 of the 1,800 shares that were bought on 1/12/2001 for £5.10 each (shares bought in the 30 days after disposal). This leaves 800 of that purchase to join the pool.

2. Matching of the 15/8/2024 disposal of 2,500 shares will be entirely against the pool, since there were no shares of that type bought on that date or the following 30 days.

3. We will first need to build up the pool to August 2024, so that we can calculate the balances.

		Number	Cost £
1/5/1985	Purchase	1,000	4,000
1/1/1990	Bonus Issue	250	
1/1/1992	Purchase	1,750	7,350
1/1/1995	Rights Issue	1,500	6,150
1/12/2001	Balance of Purchase (1,800 *less* 1,000 already matched)	800	4,080
		5,300	21,580
15/8/2024	Disposal	(2,500)	(10,179)*
	Pool balance after disposal	2,800	11,401

*The cost of the shares disposed of is calculated as:

(2,500 / 5,300) x £21,580 = £10,179

We can now calculate the gain on the disposal of shares, using the cost figure calculated in the pool.

	£
Proceeds	25,000
less cost	(10,179)
Gain	14,821

4 This task involves the computations on other asset disposals.

Land

	£
Proceeds	20,000
less apportioned cost:	
£15,000 x £20,000 / £60,000	(5,000)
Gain	15,000

Antique Ring

	£
Proceeds	6,600
less cost	(3,500)
Provisional gain	3,100

Gain is limited to 5/3 (£6,600 – £6,000) = £1,000

Antique Painting

	£
Proceeds	10,000
less cost	(14,000)
Loss	(4,000)

5

	£
Gains	
Shares	14,821
Land	15,000
Antique ring	1,000
	30,821
less loss on antique painting	(4,000)
Net gains	26,821
less exempt amount	(3,000)
Subject to CGT	23,821
Capital Gains Tax	
£8,500 x 10%	850.00
£15,321 x 20%	3,064.20
	3,914.20

Chapter Summary

- Capital Gains Tax is assessable on individuals who dispose of chargeable assets during the tax year. A disposal usually takes the form of the sale or gift of the asset. All assets are chargeable unless they are exempt. Exempt assets include main residences, cars, government securities (gilts), and certain chattels.

- Each disposal uses a separate computation that compares the proceeds or market value with the original cost of the asset.

- Losses are set off against gains. An annual exempt amount is deductible from the net gains. The balance is taxed at 10% or 20% depending on the individual's income.

- The cost of a part disposal is calculated by apportioning the cost of the whole asset. This is carried out by using the proceeds of the part disposed of as a proportion of the value of the whole asset at the time of disposal.

- Improvement expenditure that is reflected in the asset when disposed of is an allowable cost.

- Main residences are exempt assets provided they are occupied as such during the whole ownership. Certain periods of absence are treated as deemed periods of occupation. Where there are periods of absence that do not fall under these special rules, the exempt part of the gain on the property is calculated as a proportion of the whole gain, based on the period of occupation as a fraction of the period of ownership.

- Chattels that are acquired and sold for under £6,000 are exempt. Where they are sold at a gain for over £6,000 the gain is restricted to 5/3 of the gross proceeds minus £6,000. Where sold at a loss for under £6,000, the loss is restricted by substituting £6,000 for the actual proceeds in the computation.

- When shares of the same type in the same company are bought and sold at different times, matching rules are used to identify the shares disposed of. Firstly, shares bought on the day of disposal are matched. Secondly, those bought in the 30 days after disposal are matched. Thirdly, any earlier acquisitions are pooled and matched. This is known as the FA 1985 pool.

- Bonus and rights issues are treated as acquired at the time of the shares that they are derived from for matching purposes. They normally appear as part of the FA 1985 pool.

Key Terms

Capital Gains Tax (CGT) — a tax that applies to individuals who dispose of chargeable assets

disposal — a disposal for CGT purposes is the sale, gift, loss or destruction of an asset

chargeable asset — this term is used to describe assets whose disposal can result in a CGT liability – all assets are chargeable unless they are exempt

exempt asset — an asset that is not chargeable to CGT: exempt assets include main residences, cars, gilts, and some chattels

chattel — a tangible, moveable asset – i.e. the majority of personal possessions

wasting chattel — a chattel with an expected life of fewer than 50 years

annual exempt amount — the amount (also known as the 'annual exemption') that is deductible from an individual's net gains in a tax year before CGT is payable – the amount is £3,000 in 2024/25

net proceeds — the proceeds from the sale of an asset, less any incidental costs of selling the asset

capital loss — a capital loss results when the allowable costs of an asset exceed the sale proceeds (or market value). A loss is used by setting it against a gain in the same year, or if this is not possible, by carrying the loss forward to set against gains in the next available tax year

connected person — normally a close relative; sales to a connected person at less than market value are deemed to be at market value

part disposal — occurs when part of an asset is disposed of, but the remainder is retained

improvement expenditure — capital expenditure that enhances an asset – if the enhancement is still evident at disposal, then the improvement expenditure is an allowable cost

deemed occupation — periods of absence from a main residence that are treated as periods of occupation for CGT purposes

matching rules for shares — rules which determine which acquisitions of shares are identified with each disposal

bonus shares — extra shares given to shareholders in proportion to their current shareholding

rights issue — shares sold to existing shareholders at a special preferential price

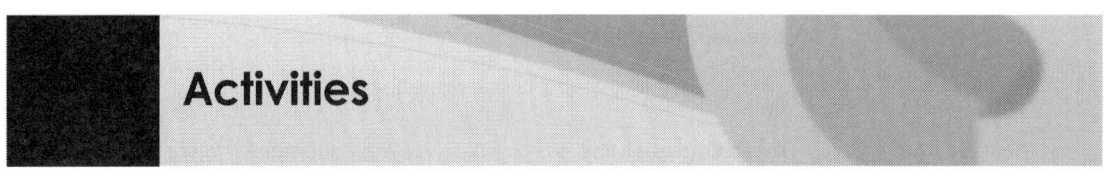

Activities

6.1 Analyse the following list of assets into those that are chargeable to CGT and those that are exempt.

		Chargeable	Exempt
(a)	An antique painting sold for £10,000		
(b)	An individual's second home, used for weekends away		
(c)	Shares in CIC plc		
(d)	An individual's only home		
(e)	A small yacht		
(f)	An antique bed, bought for £500, and sold for £2,000		
(g)	A car		
(h)	Government securities		

6.2 Josie had a capital gain on her only disposal in the tax year of £15,000. It was not a gain on residential property. Her taxable income is £22,000.

Calculate the amount of Josie's Capital Gains Tax liability for the tax year.

6.3 Tariq had a capital gain on one disposal in the tax year of £35,000, and on the only other disposal, a capital loss of £9,000. Neither disposals were on residential property. His taxable income is £28,200 (after deducting personal allowance).

Calculate the amount of Tariq's Capital Gains Tax liability for the tax year.

6.4 April bought an asset in May 1995 for £60,000 and sold it in the current tax year for £130,000. She had no other disposals in the current tax year. April is a higher rate Income Tax payer.

Calculate April's CGT liability for the tax year.

6.5 Cliff bought a field in August 1998 for £50,000 and sold it in the tax year for £165,000. In the same month he sold some shares for £32,000 which he had bought in July 2004 for £52,000. Cliff has taxable income of £40,000.

Calculate Cliff's CGT liability for the tax year.

Capital Gains Tax

6.6 Ivan Asset has capital losses brought forward from the previous tax year of £15,000. He made the following disposals during the tax year.

He sold his entire holding of 5,000 shares that he owned in Astro plc for £12.00 each. He had bought all the shares in June 1998 for £8.00 each.

He sold his Morgan car for £15,000. He had owned the car since January 1999 when he had bought it for £29,000.

He sold an antique dresser for £14,000 that he had bought in July 1996 for £9,000.

He gave his son 4,000 shares in Expo Ltd. He bought all the shares in January 1995 for £2.00 each. The shares were valued at £5 each at the time of the gift.

Ivan is a higher rate Income Tax payer.

Required:

(a) Calculate any gain or loss arising from each of the disposals.

(b) Calculate the amount of Capital Gains Tax payable for the tax year.

6.7 Justin Shaw has capital losses brought forward from the previous tax year of £18,000. He made the following disposals during the tax year. Justin's taxable income is £25,000:

He sold his yacht for £12,000. He had owned it since January 2001 when he had bought it for £23,000.

He sold his entire holding of 1,000 shares that he owned in Captain plc for £15.00 each. He had bought all the shares in June 1997 for £9.00 each.

He sold an antique painting of a ship for £14,000 that he had bought in July 1984 for £10,000.

He gave his daughter 3,000 shares in Boater Ltd. He bought all the shares in January 1996 for £3.00 each. The shares were valued at £7 each at the time of the gift.

Required:

(a) Calculate any gain or loss arising from each of the disposals.

(b) Calculate the amount of Capital Gains Tax payable for the tax year.

6.8 For each statement, tick the appropriate box.

		Actual proceeds used	Deemed proceeds used	No gain or loss basis
(a)	Grandfather gives an asset to his granddaughter			
(b)	Wife gives an asset to her husband			
(c)	Steve sells an asset to his friend for £13,000 when the market value is £16,000			
(d)	Mary sells an asset to her son's wife for £20,000 when the market value is £60,000			
(e)	Sue gives an asset to her civil partner, April			

6.9 (1) Andrew bought an asset in January 2000 for £26,000, selling it in the current tax year for £45,000. He paid auctioneers commission of 3% when he bought the asset and 5% when he sold the asset.

The gain on this asset is:

(a)	£20,470	
(b)	£15,970	
(c)	£17,530	
(d)	£19,000	

(2) True or false: advertising costs are not an allowable deduction as they are revenue expenses.

6.10 State which of the following statements are true:

(1) The annual exemption is applied before capital losses are deducted.

(2) Excess capital losses cannot be set against other taxable income.

(3) Capital gains are taxed at 20% for basic rate tax payers.

6.11 Alice made the following disposals in the tax year. She is a higher rate Income Tax payer.

She sold part of a piece of land for £30,000 that she had bought in January 1992. The whole piece of land had cost her £50,000 at that time. At the time of the sale the remaining land was valued at £120,000.

She sold her antique painting for £300,000 that she had bought for £60,000 in September 1985. She had also spent £50,000 in January 1992 having the painting restored.

Required:

Calculate the total Capital Gains Tax for Alice for the tax year.

6.12 Bertie made the following disposals in the tax year. Bertie's taxable income is £20,000.

He sold an antique painting for £20,000 that he had bought for £5,000 in January 1992. He had the painting professionally restored in January 1995, and this cost £6,000.

He sold an antique table for £7,800. The table had been bought in January 1990 for £1,400. Selling costs were £100.

Required:

Calculate the total Capital Gains Tax for Bertie for the tax year.

6.13 Christine made the following disposals in the tax year.

She gave her sister an antique necklace that she had bought for £5,000. The necklace was valued at £8,000 at the time of the gift.

She sold her Jaguar E-type car for £18,000. She had bought the car for £6,000, and spent £10,000 having it professionally restored.

On 31/12/2024 she sold her house in Dorking for £470,000. The house had been bought for £80,000 on 1/1/1997. Her use of the house was as follows:

1/1/1997 - 31/12/2006	occupied as Christine's main home
1/1/2007 - 31/12/2008	rented out as Christine went on a world holiday
1/1/2009 - 31/12/2017	occupied as Christine's main home
1/1/2018 - 31/12/2024	rented out as Christine moved to a new house.

Required:

Calculate the total taxable gains for Christine for the tax year.

6.14 David made the following disposals in the tax year. He is a higher rate Income Tax payer.

He sold 14,400 of his ordinary shares in Zydeco Ltd on 30/07/2024 for £72,000 in total. His shareholding in this company had been built up as follows:

1/1/1992	Bought 3,000 shares for £3.00 each
1/1/1999	Bought 12,000 shares for £3.50 each
1/1/2000	Bought rights issue shares on the basis of 1 for 5 at the price of £2.00 each

David sold an antique dresser for £6,900. The dresser was bought for £3,000 in January 2000.

Required:

Calculate any gain made on:

- the disposal of shares in July 2024, and
- the disposal of the dresser

Calculate the amount of any CGT that will be payable.

6.15 Edward is a higher rate Income Tax payer. Edward had acquired the following quoted ordinary shares in Exray Plc (a listed company):

1/5/1985	1,000 shares	£8,000
1/1/1992	1,750 shares	£15,750
1/1/1995	1,500 shares	£10,650 (Rights issue)
1/12/2001	1,800 shares	£18,360

On 15/11/2001 he sold 2,000 of his shareholding.

On 15/7/2024 he sold a further 2,500 ordinary shares in Exray Plc for £12.00 each.

Edward also made the following disposals during the tax year:

- he sold a plot of land for £20,000. This originally formed part of a larger field that he bought for £5,000 in January 1988. At the date of disposal the remaining portion of land was valued at £80,000
- he sold an antique brooch for £9,600. He had bought it on 1 January 1999 for £5,500
- he sold an antique table for £12,000. He had bought it on 1 December 1999 for £13,500

Required:

(1) Identify which shares would have already been matched against the disposal that took place on 15/11/2001.

(2) Show how the disposal of shares on 15/7/2024 will be matched against the acquisitions, and

(3) Calculate the total gain arising from the sale of shares that took place on 15/7/2024.

(4) Calculate any gains or losses arising from the disposal of the other assets.

(5) Calculate the total Capital Gains Tax payable in respect of the tax year.

Capital Gains Tax

6.16 Robert bought a house on 1 February 2009 for £70,000. He lived in the house until 31 January 2014 when he moved in with his elderly parents. The house remained unoccupied until he sold it on 1 July 2024 for £205,000. This house is Robert's only property.

(a) Which periods are treated as occupied and which are not?

Occupation / Deemed Occupation	Non-occupation

(b) What is the chargeable gain on the property?

6.17 The following table relates to sales of chattels.

Match the statements shown below to the correct asset details.

Asset	Sale proceeds	Cost	Statement
1	£4,000	£3,000	
2	£12,000	£8,000	
3	£7,000	£5,000	
4	£3,000	£8,000	
5	£15,000	£21,000	

Statements:

Exempt asset

Calculate gain as normal

Calculate loss as normal

Sale proceeds to be £6,000

Chattel marginal relief applies

7 Inheritance Tax

this chapter covers...

In this chapter we will examine the basic features of the rather complex topic of Inheritance Tax, which can apply to an individual's estate (net assets) left at death, and to some lifetime gifts.

We will start by explaining the various types of transfer and their implications. We will then see how an individual's estate can be charged to Inheritance Tax after they have died.

Next we will study lifetime transfers; gifts that are exempt, those that are chargeable, and those that are potentially exempt. Potentially exempt transfers will become exempt if the individual lives for at least seven years after making the transfer. We will see how all these types of transfers can affect Inheritance Tax.

We complete the chapter by looking at the special rules that can be applied at death relating to taper relief and gifts to charity.

OVERVIEW

Inheritance Tax (or IHT) can apply to the 'estate' of an individual who has died, and can also sometimes apply to gifts that an individual makes during their lifetime. Both these are known as 'transfers' – either transfers on death or lifetime transfers.

impact of domicile

Individuals who are UK domiciled (see Chapter 1) are subject to Inheritance Tax on property anywhere in the world. Non UK domiciled individuals are generally chargeable to Inheritance Tax only on property within the UK. Notice that there is a broad similarity between these rules and the ones we discussed earlier for income and gains. In certain circumstances individuals that are not UK domiciled can elect to be treated for Inheritance Tax purposes as if they were UK domiciled.

types of transfer

We need to understand the different types of 'transfer' for Inheritance Tax purposes, and what the implications are, as follows:

- **exempt transfers** – these are not chargeable to Inheritance Tax and can be excluded from any calculations. Some types of exempt transfers only relate to lifetime transfers, whilst others could be made either during the lifetime or at death.

- **chargeable lifetime transfers** – these transfers are subject to Inheritance Tax as soon as they are carried out. Those that exceed the cumulative tax threshold (or 'nil rate band') of £325,000 will involve payment of Inheritance Tax. We will see exactly how the tax threshold works shortly. The main category of chargeable lifetime transfers are transfers into specific trusts.

- **potentially exempt transfers** – these are lifetime transfers that will be exempt from Inheritance Tax if the donor (the individual making the gift) lives for at least seven years after the gift is made. All lifetime transfers except exempt transfers and chargeable lifetime transfers are potentially exempt transfers – sometimes known as PETs.

- **transfers on death** – when an individual dies, their 'estate' is made up of the assets that they owned minus any liabilities and funeral expenses. On death the individual is treated as making a final transfer of the whole of his or her estate.

TRANSFERS ON DEATH

We will start our explanation of how Inheritance Tax works by looking just at transfers made on death. Later on we can see how previous lifetime transfers by the same individual can affect the amount of Inheritance Tax.

There is a tax threshold of £325,000. **If there were no lifetime transfers**, the Inheritance Tax at death is normally calculated as follows:

- calculate the value of the estate
- deduct any exempt transfers
- deduct the tax threshold of £325,000
- calculate Inheritance Tax at **40%** on any balance

Where the estate includes the individual's home, and this is passed to a direct descendant, an additional threshold of up to £175,000 can apply. We will look at the details of how this works a little later in the chapter.

The payment of Inheritance Tax relating to death is the responsibility of the **executor** of the individual's will (if there is a will), or the **administrator** of the estate if there is no will. An executor is a person (there can be more than one) that is named in the will with responsibility for dealing with the estate. In order to pay the Inheritance Tax, the executor or administrator will use money from the estate before it is distributed to the beneficiaries.

exempt transfers on death

The following are the main transfers made on death that are exempt from Inheritance Tax. The transfers are usually made because they are bequests stated in the individual's will.

- transfers to a UK domiciled **spouse** (husband or wife) or **civil partner**
- transfers to **charities**
- transfers to **qualifying political parties**
- transfers for **national purposes** (eg to universities, museums or National Trust)

Inheritance Tax computations

Through this chapter on Inheritance Tax we will use some computations to demonstrate how the system works. In the next case study, we will show how the tax is calculated, and later on we will use further case studies and activities to help with understanding of various issues.

Although it is currently unlikely that you will be asked to carry out an Inheritance Tax computation in your examination, it is vital that you understand the principles of the tax. This understanding can be developed by following closely the way that the tax is calculated, and how the various reliefs that are available are incorporated into the computations.

Case Study

JOHN ABEL:
INHERITANCE TAX ON DEATH

situation

John Abel died, leaving an estate valued at £1,000,000. John did not own a house. He had made no lifetime transfers. In his will he left £600,000 to his wife, Susan, £5,000 to charity, and the balance of his estate to be divided equally between his two children, William and Mary. The executor of the will was John's brother, Nigel.

required

- Calculate the amount of Inheritance Tax payable.
- Calculate the amount to be received by William and Mary.
- State who is responsible for paying the Inheritance Tax.

solution

Calculation of Inheritance Tax:

	£
Total value of estate	1,000,000
less exempt transfers:	
to Susan (spouse)	(600,000)
to charity	(5,000)
	395,000
less nil rate band	(325,000)
	70,000
Inheritance Tax 40% of £70,000	28,000

Calculation of amount to be received by William and Mary:

	£
Total value of estate	1,000,000
less transfers to Susan and to charity	(605,000)
less Inheritance Tax	(28,000)
Balance of estate to be shared	367,000

William and Mary will receive £183,500 each.

The executor of the estate, Nigel, will be responsible for paying the Inheritance Tax, but the money will come from the estate. The Inheritance Tax will effectively reduce the value of the estate and hence the amount received by William and Mary.

transfer of unused threshold

Where an individual dies and the £325,000 nil rate band (or part of it) is not used, the individual's spouse or civil partner can subsequently add the unused part to their own nil rate band.

residence nil rate band (RNRB)

This additional threshold (of up to £175,000 in 2024/25) can apply to transfers on death when the estate includes a home which the individual has used as his or her residence. The home (or part of it) must be left to the individual's direct descendants. This includes children and grandchildren and their spouses or civil partners.

The additional threshold will be the lower of:

- The value of the home or share in it that direct descendants inherit, and
- £175,000

The additional threshold will be deducted in the calculation of Inheritance Tax on death, just before the main nil rate band is applied. It cannot apply to lifetime transfers.

PETER SMITH: RESIDENCE NIL RATE BAND

situation

Peter Smith died, leaving a home worth £350,000, plus other assets valued at £190,000, all to his grandson.

required

Calculate the amount of Inheritance Tax payable.

solution

	£
Total value of estate	540,000
less residence nil rate band	(175,000)
less nil rate band	(325,000)
Balance subject to Inheritance Tax	40,000
Inheritance Tax 40% of £40,000	16,000

transfer of unused RNRB

Where the home is worth less than £175,000, the additional threshold will be limited to the value of the home. If the individual's spouse died later, then they could use the previously unused proportion of the residence nil rate band.

example

Mary died and left a flat (which she had lived in) valued at £131,250 to her son, David, and the remainder of her estate to her husband, Norman. The transfer to David would be covered by the RNRB, and the transfer to her husband, Norman would be exempt.

If Norman died later, leaving his home to his grandchild, he could use the 1/4 unused RNRB (currently £43,750) from Mary's death together with his own RNRB. He would also have the £325,000 normal nil rate band from Mary's death to use, together with his own.

Where a death does not use any of the residence nil rate band – for example if all the estate is left to a spouse or civil partner (or even if a home was not owned by the deceased) – then the whole RNRB can be used on the death of the spouse or civil partner. This would only apply, of course, if the second death involved leaving a home to a direct descendant. The amount of transferred RNRB will be based on the date of the second death, and so will be £175,000 if the second death occurs in 2024/25, regardless of when the first death occurred.

example

Frank died, and left his whole estate, valued at £400,000 to his wife, Cynthia. There would be no Inheritance Tax, because the transfer to a spouse is exempt.

Cynthia died later, leaving an estate valued at £800,000, including a home valued at £500,000. The entire estate was left to her daughter Susan.

Cynthia's transfer on death could use both Frank's unused RNRB and her own, each of £175,000. The transfer could also utilise both normal nil rate bands of up to £325,000 each. A maximum of £175,000 + £175,000 + £325,000 + £325,000 = £1,000,000 would therefore be available at nil rate, which would mean that no Inheritance Tax was payable on the estate of £800,000.

LIFETIME TRANSFERS

As noted earlier, lifetime transfers may be exempt, chargeable, or potentially exempt. We will start by looking at the lifetime transfers that are exempt from Inheritance Tax.

exempt transfers

All the exempt transfers on death are also exempt if made as gifts during the individual's lifetime:

- transfers to a UK domiciled **spouse** (husband or wife) or **civil partner**
- transfers to **charities**
- transfers to **qualifying political parties**
- transfers for **national purposes** (eg to universities, museums or National Trust)

In addition, the following transfers are exempt when made during the individual's lifetime:

- up to **£3,000** worth of gifts given away each tax year. This is known as the annual exemption. Any unused part of the annual exemption can be carried forward – but only for one tax year, and is used after the annual exemption for that later year

- small gifts are exempt up to **£250 per person in a tax year**. This exemption cannot be carried forward or transferred, or used in conjunction with another exempt transfer
- **marriage gifts** are exempt, up to the following amounts:
  - £5,000 given by a parent
  - £2,500 given by a grandparent
  - £2,500 given by one of the individuals getting married
  - £1,000 by anyone else
- **payments to help with living costs of:**
  - ex-spouse or civil partner
  - dependent relative who is old, ill or disabled
  - a child

example

Rachel made no gifts in the last tax year, but in the current tax year she gave the following:

- £2,900 to her son, David when he got married
- £150 to each of six grandchildren on their birthdays
- £6,000 to her daughter, Ella to help her with a house deposit

The gifts to David and the six grandchildren would all be exempt under the marriage and small gifts exemptions. The current year and previous year annual exemption can both be set against the gift to Ella, making all £6,000 exempt.

chargeable lifetime transfers

Where a chargeable lifetime transfer is made (for example to certain trusts), Inheritance Tax will become immediately due if it (together with any other chargeable transfers in the last seven years) exceeds the £325,000 nil rate band. The annual allowances (where available) are deducted before checking whether the nil rate band is exceeded. The tax rate applied to the excess is **20%**, and is paid by the recipient of the transfer (for example on behalf of the trust).

If the chargeable transfers (including those in the previous seven years) are less than £325,000 then no Inheritance Tax will be due straight away, but part (or all) of the nil rate band will be used up. That means if the individual dies within the next seven years there will be less nil rate band to set against their estate.

example

Kelly made a transfer to a trust of £400,000 that was classed as a chargeable lifetime transfer. Kelly had made no other lifetime transfers. She could deduct two £3,000 annual exemptions, leaving a chargeable transfer of £394,000. The trust would pay Inheritance Tax of (£394,000 – £325,000) x 20% = £13,800.

If the individual who made the transfer subsequently dies within seven years of the date of the transfer, their nil rate band will be reduced or eliminated by the chargeable transfer. At death, the tax on the chargeable transfer would also be re-calculated at the 40% rate, so that the receiver of the transfer would need to pay any additional tax due.

example

To continue the earlier example, if Kelly died two years after making the transfer, Inheritance Tax would be re-calculated on the transfer at 40% instead of the 20% already paid. This additional tax of £13,800 would be borne by the trust that received the transfer. This calculation is (£394,000 – £325,000) x 40%, minus £13,800 already paid.

The chargeable lifetime transfer was within seven years of her death, and it used up all her nil rate band. If Kelly's estate at death was valued at £500,000 (with no exempt transfers and no home), Inheritance Tax of £500,000 x 40% = £200,000 would be payable from the estate.

potentially exempt transfers (PETs)

Lifetime transfers that are neither exempt nor chargeable are potentially exempt transfers. There is no immediate charge to Inheritance Tax when a potentially exempt transfer is made. If the individual who made that transfer lives for **at least seven years after the date of the transfer**, there is **no** impact on Inheritance Tax at all. The **potentially** exempt transfer will have become **exempt**.

When an individual has died, any potentially exempt transfers that he or she made in the previous seven years will be counted in the Inheritance Tax calculation. These transfers will therefore use up some (or all) of the nil rate band, and could become subject to Inheritance Tax at 40%. If the PET exceeds the cumulative nil rate band the recipient is liable for the IHT. The calculation is carried out in chronological order, with the estate making up the final transfer.

Inheritance Tax **167**

> **example**
>
> Suppose Brian gave £50,000 to his daughter to help her buy her first house. If he had made no other transfers in the current or previous tax year he could deduct two £3,000 annual exemptions from the gift, leaving a potentially exempt transfer of £44,000. No Inheritance Tax would be due at this point.
>
> If Brian died two years later, leaving an estate valued at £350,000 (with no exempt transfers and no home), the Inheritance Tax would be calculated as follows:
>
> | | £ |
> | --- | ---: |
> | Potentially exempt transfer – now chargeable | 44,000 |
> | Nil rate band | 325,000 |
> | Nil rate band available against estate | 281,000 |
> | Estate | 350,000 |
> | *less* nil rate band balance (as above) | 281,000 |
> | Chargeable to tax | 69,000 |
> | IHT 40% of £69,000 | 27,600 |
>
> The IHT would all relate to the estate, since the gift to Brian's daughter would be set against the nil rate band before the estate.

We will now use a Case Study to see how all the types of transfer together impact on Inheritance Tax.

Case Study

JENNY RUSH:
LIFETIME AND DEATH TRANSFERS

situation

Jenny (who had not made any transfers the previous tax year) made the following lifetime transfers:

31 May 2023	£150,000 payment into a trust (a chargeable transfer)
30 June 2023	£60,000 to her son, Jonah to pay for his university fees
30 Sept 2023	£4,000 to her daughter, Isabel when she got married

On 31 December 2024, Jenny died and left an estate valued at £650,000. The estate did not include a home. Jenny's will listed the following beneficiaries:

- £300,000 to be paid to her husband, Wilf
- £10,000 to be paid to charity
- The balance to be shared equally between Jonah and Isabel

required

Calculate the:

- Inheritance Tax payable during Jenny's lifetime
- Inheritance Tax payable on Jenny's death

solution

Inheritance Tax payable during lifetime:

Two £3,000 annual exemptions can be set against the chargeable transfer of £150,000, leaving £144,000. As this is below the £325,000 threshold there is no Inheritance Tax to pay during Jenny's lifetime.

Inheritance Tax payable on death:

The lifetime gift to Jonah of £60,000 is a potentially exempt transfer that has become chargeable at death.

The lifetime gift to Isabel is exempt under the marriage gift rules.

The nil rate band available at death is calculated as:

	£
Original nil rate band	325,000
less Chargeable Lifetime Transfer	(144,000)
less PET now chargeable	(60,000)
Nil rate band available against estate	121,000

Inheritance Tax at death:

		£
Estate at death		650,000
less exempt transfers	to husband Wilf	(300,000)
	to charity	(10,000)
less nil rate band available (calculated above)		(121,000)
Subject to Inheritance Tax		219,000
Inheritance Tax at 40%		87,600

TAPERING RELIEF

Where lifetime transfers have been made, and Inheritance Tax is subsequently due on these transfers at death, there can be a reduction in tax. If the lifetime transfer was made between three and seven years before death, the amount of Inheritance Tax due on death will be as follows:

Time between transfer and death	% of normal tax due
3 to 4 years	80%
4 to 5 years	60%
5 to 6 years	40%
6 to 7 years	20%

These rates will only apply where the lifetime transfers exceed the nil rate band of £325,000, resulting in IHT becoming payable on death.

example

The only lifetime transfer made by Rashid was a PET of £375,000 (after exemptions) made on 30 September 2020. If Rashid subsequently died on 15 October 2024 (between four and five years after the transfer), the Inheritance Tax due relating to the PET would be calculated as:

	£
PET now chargeable	375,000
less nil rate band	(325,000)
Chargeable to Inheritance Tax	50,000
Inheritance Tax £50,000 x 40% x 60%	12,000

This IHT would be payable by the recipient of the PET.

His estate would then all be charged at the normal rate of 40% (with no reduction). The nil rate band would have been used up.

GIFTS AT DEATH TO CHARITY

As already stated, gifts to charities in lifetime or on death are exempt. In addition, if 10% or more of the 'net value' of an estate is given to charity, then the normal rate of 40% Inheritance Tax can be reduced to 36%. The net value is calculated after deducting the nil rate band, the residence nil rate band and other exempt transfers (for example to a spouse).

example

Sophie died and left a total estate of £900,000. It did not include a home. Of this, £200,000 was left to her civil partner, and £40,000 to charity.

The net estate would equal £900,000 – £200,000 – £325,000 = £375,000.

10% would equal 37,500. Since the gift to charity of £40,000 was more than this, the Inheritance Tax would be calculated at 36%, not 40%. IHT would be calculated as (£375,000 – £40,000 = £335,000) x 36% = £120,600.

PAYMENT OF INHERITANCE TAX

The normal due dates of payment are as follows:

- for chargeable lifetime transfers made between 6 April and 30 September the IHT is payable by 30 April in the following year

- for chargeable lifetime transfers made between 1 October and 5 April the IHT is payable six months after the end of the month in which the transfer was made

- for transfers on death (including additional tax due on chargeable lifetime transfers and tax on PETs that have become chargeable) the tax is payable six months after the end of the month in which death occurred

Chapter Summary

- Inheritance Tax is charged on death estates and some lifetime transfers that exceed a cumulative nil rate band (or threshold) of £325,000.
- An additional threshold of up to £175,000 can apply on death where a home is left to a direct descendant or their spouse.
- For Inheritance Tax purposes there are several types of transfer; exempt transfers, chargeable lifetime transfers, potentially exempt transfers, and transfers on death.
- The only lifetime transfers that incur Inheritance Tax immediately are Chargeable Lifetime Transfers that (together with any in the previous seven years) exceed the £325,000 nil rate band.
- Potentially exempt transfers (PETs) are lifetime transfers which are not exempt or chargeable. If the donor survives seven years after the gift, these transfers become exempt. If the donor does not survive seven years, these transfers are accounted for at death. The recipient is then liable for any IHT on the PET where it exceeds the cumulative nil rate band.
- Unused nil rate band amounts can be passed on to a spouse or civil partner.
- Tax at death on potentially exempt transfers that have become chargeable, and chargeable lifetime transfers, can be reduced if they occurred between three and seven years before death.
- Gifts to charity at death can reduce the tax rate if the gifts exceed 10% of the net estate.

Key Terms

Inheritance Tax (IHT) — a tax that is applied to death estates and some lifetime transfers where a cumulative threshold is exceeded

residence nil rate band — an additional threshold that can apply on death where a home is left to a direct descendant

exempt transfers — transfers, either during the lifetime or at death, that are not counted for Inheritance Tax purposes

chargeable lifetime transfers — transfers, mainly to certain trusts, that can incur an immediate IHT charge

potentially exempt transfers (PETs) — lifetime gifts that will become exempt if the donor survives at least seven years from the date of the gift

death estate — the value of an individual's assets minus liabilities that form a final transfer upon death

Tapering Relief — the reduced rate of IHT at death related to lifetime transfers where they occur between three and seven years before death

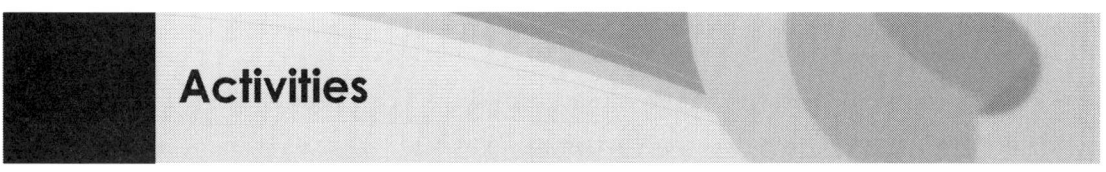

Activities

7.1 Theo died, leaving an estate of £595,000 with no home. He had not made any lifetime transfers. In his will he left the following:

£200,000 to his wife, Sophie.

£2,000 to a qualifying political party.

The balance of his estate to his daughter, Jane.

Calculate the Inheritance Tax due on the estate, and how much Jane will receive.

7.2 Angela and Tony had been married for many years, when Tony died. Tony had not made any lifetime transfers. In Tony's will he left £20,000 to each of their three adult sons, and the balance to Angela. Tony's estate was valued at £300,000. It did not include a home.

Two years after Tony's death, Angela died. She had not made any lifetime transfers. Her estate was valued at £950,000, including a home valued at £350,000, which was to be divided equally between her three sons.

Calculate the Inheritance Tax (if any) due on Angela's estate.

7.3 Examine the following list of transfers and identify which are only exempt for lifetime transfers, and which are exempt for both lifetime and death transfers.

Exempt Transfers		Only for Lifetime Transfers	Lifetime or Death Transfers
(a)	Gifts of up to £3,000 in total		
(b)	Transfers to spouse		
(c)	Gifts to museums		
(d)	Gifts to individuals of up to £250		
(e)	Gifts to charities		
(f)	Gifts to qualifying political parties		

7.4 Vikram made the following gifts during the current tax year. He had already used up the previous year's annual exemption.

- £200 was given to each of his six grandchildren.
- A ring worth £5,000 was given to his wife.
- A gift of £2,500 was made to a friend who was in financial difficulties.
- A gift costing £800 was given to a friend's daughter when she got married.
- Sports equipment costing £1,200 was given to a local charity.

For each gift, state whether it will be exempt, and if so state the relevant exemption rule.

7.5 Mervyn (who had not made any transfers in recent tax years) made the following lifetime transfers:

31 January 2023	£220,000 payment into a trust (a chargeable transfer)
30 April 2023	£25,000 to his daughter, Josie
30 June 2023	£25,000 to his daughter, June on her 21st birthday

On 31 October 2024, Mervyn died and left an estate valued at £720,000, including a home worth £220,000. Mervyn's will listed the following beneficiaries:

- £325,000 to be paid to his wife, Julie
- £8,000 to be given to a qualifying political party

The balance, including the home, to be shared equally between Josie and June.

Required:

Calculate the:

- Inheritance Tax payable during Mervyn's lifetime
- Inheritance Tax payable on Mervyn's death

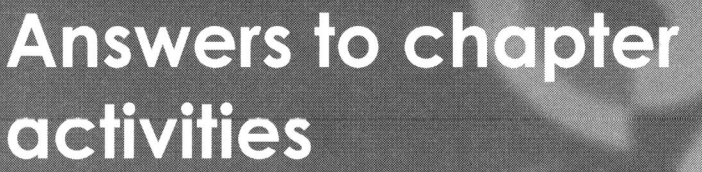

Answers to chapter activities

CHAPTER 1: INTRODUCTION TO TAXATION

1.1 (a), (c) and (f) are false; (b), (d) and (e) are true.

1.2 The following statements are true: (a), (e), (f). The other statements are false.

1.3 Income Tax Computation for Mary

	£	£ Tax Paid
Trading Income	2,800	–
Employment Income	12,300	–
Property Income	4,500	–
Total Income	19,600	0
less Personal Allowance	12,570	
Taxable Income	7,030	
Income Tax Calculation:		
£7,030 x 20%	1,406.00	
Income Tax Liability	1,406.00	
less already paid	0.00	
Income Tax to pay	1,406.00	

Note:

The employment income is based on the amount received in the tax year, irrespective of the period that it relates to.

1.4 **(a)** Dividend Income, part of Savings and Investment Income

(b) Employment Income – full title Employment, Pensions and Social Security Income

(c) Exempt

(d) Savings Income, part of Savings and Investment Income

(e) Exempt

(f) Property Income

1.5 Income Tax Computation for John

	£	£ Tax Paid
Employment Income	10,800	0
Property Income	6,000	–
Total Income	16,800	0
less Personal Allowance	12,570	
Taxable Income	4,230	
Income Tax Calculation:		
£4,230 x 20%	846.00	
Income Tax Liability	846.00	
less already paid	0.00	
Income Tax to pay	846.00	

Note:

The interest on an ISA is exempt.

1.6 Income Tax Computation for Megan

	£	£
		Tax Paid
Trading Income	24,700	–
Employment Income	34,400	4,366
Total Income	59,100	4,366
less Personal Allowance	12,570	
Taxable Income	46,530	
Income Tax Calculation:		
£37,700 x 20%	7,540.00	
£8,830 x 40%	3,532.00	
£46,530		
Income Tax Liability	11,072.00	
less already paid	4,366.00	
Income Tax to pay	6,706.00	

Note:

The employment income is based on the amount received in the tax year, irrespective of the period that it relates to.

1.7 **(a)**, **(b)** and **(d)** are true; **(c)**, **(e)** and **(f)** are false.

1.8 Applying the 'automatic not resident test', Chloe is not a UK resident for 2024/25. She works full time overseas, spends fewer than 91 days in the UK, and works in the UK for fewer than 31 days.

1.9 Bernard is not a UK resident for 2024/25. Using the ties test, an individual who is in the UK for 46 to 90 days will need at least three ties to the UK to be considered a UK resident.

answers to chapter activities

CHAPTER 2: INCOME FROM PROPERTY

2.1

	£
Rent received	5,000
Less	
Insurance (9 months at £25)	225
Replacement of fridge	200
Assessable property income for 2024/25	4,575

2.2

		£
Rental Income for period 6/11/24 - 5/4/25	(£400 x 5)	2,000
Less		
Insurance (5 months at £30)		150
Agent's Fees (£100 x 5)		500
Assessable property income for 2024/25		1,350

The legal fees relating to the purchase of the property are a capital cost.

2.3

	£	£
Rental Income Received		10,000
less allowable expenditure:		
Council Tax	700	
Water Rates	300	
Insurance	400	
Replacement of carpets	2,500	
Managing Agent's Charges	1,000	
		4,900
Assessable property income		5,100

2.4

	No 1 £	No 2 £	No 3 £	Total £
Rental Income	8,000	6,000	5,500	19,500
less allowable expenditure:				
Council Tax	800	650	400	1,850
Managing Agent's Charges	1,600	1,200	1,100	3,900
Property Insurance	400	300	250	950
Redecoration	–	600	–	600
Repainting Windows	500	450	500	1,450
Other Repairs	300	400	200	900
Accountancy Fees	150	150	150	450
Profit / (Loss)	4,250	2,250	2,900	9,400
less loss brought forward				1,000
Property Income				8,400

The council tax for property three is allowed since it relates to the period that it is occupied. Other expenses for this property relate to the period that it was owned for the business of letting and are therefore allowable. The purchase of furniture was not replacement items, and is therefore not allowable.

2.5 (1) Property Income Computation

	£	£
Rental Income Received		11,500
less allowable expenditure:		
Accountancy Fees	400	
Council Tax	650	
Water Rates	350	
Insurance	300	
Replacement of carpets	2,000	
Managing Agent's Charges	1,000	
		4,700
Property income		6,800

(2) **Income Tax Computation**

	Income £	Tax Paid £
Employment Income	49,500	7,386
Property Income	6,800	–
Total Income	56,300	7,386
less Personal Allowance	12,570	
Taxable Income	43,730	

Income Tax Calculation:

37,700 x 20%		7,540.00
6,030 x 40%		2,412.00
43,730		
	Income Tax Liability	9,952.00
	less Paid	7,386.00
	Income Tax to pay	2,566.00

2.6

	Three bedroom house £	One bedroom flat £
Income	6,300	4,500
Expenses:		
Management charge	504	
Council tax and water		1,400
Insurance		270
Profits	5,796	2,830

2.7 **(a)** and **(d)** use actual costs; **(b)** and **(c)** use property allowance

CHAPTER 3: INCOME FROM SAVINGS AND INVESTMENTS

3.1 **(d)** £2,730   Employment (£20,720 – £12,570) x 20% = £1,630

Savings (£6,500 – £1,000) x 20% = £1,100

3.2 **(a)** **Savings Income:**

£1,300

£1,000 (personal savings allowance)

―――

£300 x 20% = £60.00 tax on savings income

(b) **Dividend Income:**

£350

£350 (dividend allowance)

―――

Nil No tax due on dividends

3.3 **Income Tax Computation**

	Income £	Tax Paid £
Employment Income	29,150	3,316
Property Income	1,900	–
B/S Int	1,500	–
Dividends	1,800	–
Total Income	34,350	3,316
less Personal Allowance	12,570	
Taxable Income	21,780	

Analysis of Taxable Income:

General Income	(£29,150 + £1,900 – £12,570)	£18,480
Savings Income		£1,500
Dividend Income		£1,800
		£21,780

	Income £	Tax Paid £
Income Tax Calculation:		
General Income		
£18,480 x 20%	3,696.00	
		3,696.00
Savings Income:		
£1,000 x 0% (personal savings allowance)	0.00	
£500 x 20%	100.00	
		100.00
£1,500		
Dividend Income:		
£500 x 0% (dividend allowance)	0.00	
£1,300 x 8.75%	113.75	
£1,800		
		113.75
Income Tax Liability		3,909.75
less Paid		3,316.00
Income Tax to Pay		593.75

3.4 Income Tax Computation

	Income £	Tax Paid £
Employment Income	21,600	1,806
Savings Income	2,000	–
Dividend Income	5,500	–
Total Income	29,100	1,806
less Personal Allowance	12,570	
Taxable Income	16,530	

Analysis of Taxable Income:

General Income	(£21,600 – £12,570)	£9,030
Savings Income		£2,000
Dividend Income		£5,500
		£16,530

Income Tax Calculation:	Income £	Tax Paid £
General Income:		
£9,030 x 20%	1,806.00	
		1,806.00
Savings Income:		
£1,000 x 0% (personal savings allowance)	0.00	
£1,000 x 20%	200.00	
£2,000		200.00
Dividend Income:		
£500 x 0% (dividend allowance)	0.00	
£5,000 x 8.75%	437.50	
£5,500		
		437.50
Income Tax Liability		2,443.50
less Paid		1,806.00
Income Tax to pay		637.50

3.5 (a)

Savings Income

Date	Details	Assessable Amount
		£
30/6/24	Interest from 'gilt'	1,500.00
31/1/25	Bank of North'd	11,875.00
31/3/25	Osborne Bank	750.00
Total		14,125.00

Dividend Income

Date	Details	Assessable Amount
		£
31/5/24	Growth plc	4,000.00

Note that the interest from the ISA is exempt, and that the receipts dated 31/3/24 and 30/6/25 fall outside the tax year 2024/25.

(b)

Income Tax Computation

	Income £	Tax paid £
Employment Income	25,650	2,616
Savings Income (as above)	14,125	0
Dividend Income (as above)	4,000	0
Total Income	43,775	2,616
less Personal Allowance	12,570	
Taxable Income	31,205	

Analysis of Taxable Income:

General Income (£25,650 – £12,570)	£13,080
Savings Income	£14,125
Dividend Income	£4,000
	£31,205

Income Tax Calculation:

General Income

£13,080 x 20%	2,616.00	
		2,616.00

Savings Income:

£1,000 x 0% (personal savings allowance)	0.00	
£13,125 x 20%	2,625.00	
£14,125		2,625.00

Dividend Income:

£500 x 0% (dividend allowance)	0.00	
£3,500 x 8.75%	306.25	
£4,000		306.25

Income Tax Liability	5,547.25
less paid	2,616.00
Income Tax to pay	2,931.25

3.6 (a) Cash ISAs and stocks and shares ISAs are subject to a maximum total investment in the tax year of £20,000, (c) ISAs can only be opened by individuals who are resident in the UK and (e) The total invested in a stocks and shares ISA can subsequently be transferred to a cash ISA

CHAPTER 4: INCOME FROM EMPLOYMENT

4.1

		£
Basic salary		18,000
Commission rec'd	30/4/24	1,200
	31/7/24	1,450
	31/10/24	1,080
	31/1/25	1,250
Employment income assessable amount 2024/25		22,980

4.2 Assessable **(b), (c), (f), (g – home to work is private mileage)**

Tax-free **(a), (d – interest rate higher than official rate), (e), (h)**

4.3

		£
Basic salary		20,000
Company car (16% + 13% = 29%)	(£11,500 x 29%)	3,335
	(£27,800 x 29%)	8,062
Credit card – private expenditure		100
(fuel covered by scale charge)		
Healthcare **insurance**		730
Employment income assessable amount		32,227

4.4

	£
Basic salary	28,000
less 6% pension contribution	1,680
Pay (per P60)	26,320
Vouchers (cost to employer)	850

Excess business mileage paid

	£	£
10,000 x (60p – 45p)	1,500	
1,500 x (60p – 25p)	525	
		2,025
		29,195
less allowable expenses:		
Professional fees		(170)
Assessable amount		29,025

The hotel expenses received relate to an allowable cost, and so are exempt.

4.5

(1)

	£	£
Basic salary		50,000
less 5% pension contribution		2,500
Pay (per P60)		47,500
Company car (1)		
(£18,000 x 37% x 5/12)	2,775	
Company car (2)		
((£20,000 – £1,000) x 30% x 7/12)	3,325	
		6,100
Car fuel (car 2 only)		
(£27,800 x 30% x 7/12)		4,865
Dental treatment		500
Employment Income		58,965

(Mortgage is not assessable since interest charged is over official rate.)

(2) Income Tax computation

	Income £	Tax paid £
Employment Income	58,965	6,000
Interest	1,500	–
Dividends	1,000	–
	61,465	6,000
less personal allowance	12,570	
	48,895	

Analysis of income:

General	£46,395
Savings	£1,500
Dividends	£1,000
Total	£48,895

Tax:	£	£
General Income:		
£37,700 x 20%	7,540.00	
£8,695 x 40%	3,478.00	
£46,395		11,018.00
Savings Income:		
£500 x 0% (Personal Savings Allowance)	0.00	
£1,000 x 40%	400,00	
£1,500		400,00
Dividend Income:		
£500 x 0% (Dividend Allowance)	0.00	
£500 x 33.75%	168.75	
		168.75
Tax liability		11,586.75
less Paid		6,000.00
Balance to be paid		5,586.75

4.6

(a) Contract of service is for	Employment
(b) Contract for services is for	Self-Employment
(c) Choose work hours and charge for work done	Self-Employment
(d) No need to provide own equipment	Employment
(e) Told how, when and where to do work	Employment
(f) Can employ helper or substitute	Self-Employment
(g) Correct substandard work at own cost	Self-Employment

4.7 (1) (£24,000 + £20,000)/2 x 7/12 x 1.25% = £160 (rounded down)

(2) (c) 75,000

(3) (a) Yes, (b) Yes, (c) No

(4) (a) 5,600

(5) (a) and (d) are correct

4.8

	Nissan	Mitsubishi	Honda
Benefit % Applicable	2%	12%	31%
Benefit for Private Use of Car	£611	£3,988	£9,493
Benefit for Private Use of Fuel	£0	£3,336	£8,618
Total Assessable Benefit	£611	£7,324	£18,111
Annual Income Tax Cost	£244	£2,929	£7,244

4.9

	Primary Contributions £	Secondary Contributions £
George	64.16	150.69
Helen	270.50	606.09
Natasha	0.00	185.19
Vikram	228.96	434.97

answers to chapter activities

CHAPTER 5: PREPARING INCOME TAX COMPUTATIONS

5.1 **(a)** Gross equivalent amounts:

Gift Aid £2,000 x 100/80 = £2,500

Pension £3,040 x 100/80 = £3,800

(b) Jo will get tax relief at her highest rate (40%) on her gross payments (20% when the payments are made and the other 20% in calculating her tax). The cost of her payments after tax relief will therefore be:

Gift Aid £2,500 *less* 40% = £1,500.

Pension £3,800 *less* 40% = £2,280.

5.2

Income Tax Computation

	£	£
		Tax Paid
Property Income	9,400	–
Employment Income	30,000	3,486
Interest rec'd	5,000	–
Dividend income	12,000	–
Total Income	56,400	3,486
less Personal Allowance	12,570	
Taxable Income	43,830	

Analysis of Taxable Income:	
General Income (£9,400 + £30,000 – £12,570)	£26,830
Savings Income	£5,000
Dividend Income	£12,000
	£43,830

The basic rate band will be increased by the gross equivalent of the pension payment (£2,400 x 100/80 = £3,000). This makes the new top of the band £37,700 + £3,000 = £40,700.

Income Tax Calculation:

	£	£
General Income:		
£26,830 x 20%	5,366.00	
		5,366.00
Savings Income		
£500 x 0% (personal savings allowance)	0.00	
£4,500 x 20%	900.00	
£5,000		900.00
Dividend Income		
£500 x 0% (dividend allowance)	0.00	
£8,370 x 8.75% (to £40,700 cumulative)	732.37	
£3,130 x 33.75%	1,056.37	
£12,000		
		1,788.74
Income Tax liability		8,054.74
less paid		3,486.00
Balance to pay		4,568.74

5.3

Employment income	£46,145
Bank account interest	£630
Dividends	£3,500
less	
Gift aid payments (gross)	£(375)
Adjusted net income	£49,900

Since the adjusted net income less the personal allowance is below £37,700, John is a basic rate taxpayer, and his personal savings allowance could be up to £1,000. In this case it is £630.

5.4

(a)

	£
Rent received	6,300
less insurance	350
less replacement of carpet	700
	5,250
less loss b/f	250
Property income	5,000

Note – the actual costs of £1,050 are higher than the property allowance.

(b)

Salary	148,525
Excess mileage allowance paid	
2,000 miles x (80p – 45p)	700
less ACCA membership fee	(283)
Employment Income	148,942

(c) Income Tax Computation

	£	£
		Tax Paid
Property Income	5,000	nil
Employment Income	148,942	53,000
Savings and Investment Income:		
(interest rec'd)	1,000	–
(dividends rec'd)	1,400	–
Total Income	156,342	53,000
less Personal Allowance (eliminated)	0	
Taxable Income	156,342	
Analysis of Taxable Income:		
General Income (£5,000 + £148,942)	153,942	
Savings Income	1,000	
Dividend income	1,400	
	156,342	

Income Tax Calculation:

	£	£
General Income		
£37,700 x 20%		7,540.00
£87,440 x 40%		34,976.00
£28,802 x 45%		12,960.90
£153,942		55,476.90
Savings Income		
£1,000 x 45% (no personal savings allowance)		450.00
Dividend Income £500 x 0% (dividend allowance)		0.00
£900 x 39.35%		354.15
Income Tax liability		56,281.05
less paid		53,000.00
Balance to pay		3,281.05

5.5

	£
Employment income	110,000
Dividends	6,000
	116,000
Personal allowance	4,570
Taxable income	111,430
General Income:	
£37,700 x 20%	7,540
£67,730 x 40%	27,092
Dividend Income:	
£500 x 0%	0
£5,500 x 33.75%	1,856
Tax Liability	36,488

Workings:

Adjusted net income is £110,000 + £6,000 = £116,000.

Personal allowance is £12,570 – 50% (£116,000 – £100,000) = £4,570.

5.6 (a), (c), (e) and (f) will reduce his total Income Tax liability.

(d) will benefit him financially, but will not reduce his total Income Tax liability.

5.7

	£
Employment income	109,000
Dividends	5,000
	114,000
Personal allowance	7,070
Taxable income	106,930
General Income:	
(£37,700 + £3,000) x 20%	8,140
(£101,930* – £40,700) x 40%	24,492
Dividend Income:	
£500 x 0%	0
£4,500 x 33.75%	1,518
Tax Liability	34,150

Workings:

Adjusted net income: £109,000 + £5,000 – £3,000 = £111,000

Personal allowance: £12,570 – 50% x (£111,000 – £100,000) = £7,070

*General income: £109,000 – £7,070 = £101,930

CHAPTER 6: CAPITAL GAINS TAX

6.1 Chargeable Assets: **(a)**, **(b)**, **(c)**.

Exempt Assets: **(d)**, **(e – wasting chattel)**, **(f – chattel sold for a gain for under £6,000)**, **(g)**, **(h)**.

6.2

	£	£
Gain	15,000	
less annual exempt amount	(3,000)	
Amount subject to CGT	12,000	
Capital Gains Tax:		
£12,000 x 10% (all within basic rate band)		1,200.00

6.3

	£	£
Capital Gain	35,000	
less Capital Loss	(9,000)	
Net Gain	26,000	
less annual exempt amount	(3,000)	
Amount subject to CGT	23,000	
Capital Gains Tax:		
£9,500 x 10% (£37,700 – £28,200)		950.00
£13,500 x 20%		2,700.00
		3,650.00

6.4

	£
Proceeds	130,000
less Cost	(60,000)
Gain	70,000
Gain	70,000
less Annual exempt amount	(3,000)
Subject to CGT	67,000
Capital Gains Tax (all at 20%)	13,400

6.5

	£
Field	
Proceeds	165,000
less Cost	(50,000)
Gain	115,000
Shares	
Proceeds	32,000
less Cost	(52,000)
Loss	(20,000)
Gain on field	115,000
Loss on shares	(20,000)
Net Gain	95,000
less Annual exempt amount	(3,000)
Subject to CGT	92,000
Capital Gains Tax	
£92,000 x 20%	18,400.00

6.6

Ivan Asset

(a)

Shares in Astro plc

	£
Proceeds (5,000 x £12.00)	60,000
less cost (5,000 x £8.00)	(40,000)
Gain	20,000

Morgan Car – Exempt Asset

Antique dresser

	£
Proceeds	14,000
less cost	(9,000)
Gain	5,000

Shares in Expo Ltd

	£
Market Value (4,000 x £5.00)	20,000
less cost (4,000 x £2.00)	(8,000)
Gain	12,000

(b)

The gains can now be added together, and the loss offset.

	£
Gains	
Astro plc shares	20,000
Antique dresser	5,000
Expo Ltd shares	12,000
	37,000
less loss brought forward	(15,000)
	22,000
less annual exempt amount	(3,000)
Taxable amount	19,000
Capital Gains Tax £19,000 x 20%	3,800

6.7 Justin Shaw

(a)

Yacht – Exempt as a wasting chattel

Shares in Captain plc	£
Proceeds (1,000 x £15.00)	15,000
less cost (1,000 x £9.00)	(9,000)
Gain	6,000

Antique painting	£
Proceeds	14,000
less cost	(10,000)
Gain	4,000

Shares in Boater Ltd

	£
Market Value (3,000 x £7.00)	21,000
less cost (3,000 x £3.00)	(9,000)
Gain	12,000

(b)

	£
Gains	
Captain plc shares	6,000
Antique painting	4,000
Boater Ltd shares	12,000
	22,000
less loss brought forward	(18,000)
Balance	4,000
less annual exempt amount	(3,000)
Taxable amount	1,000
Capital Gains Tax £1,000 x 10%	£100

6.8 (a) Deemed proceeds used
(b) No gain or loss basis
(c) Actual proceeds used
(d) Deemed proceeds used
(e) No gain or loss basis

6.9 (1) (b) £15,970
(2) False

6.10 (1) False
(2) True
(3) False

6.11

	£
Land	
Proceeds	30,000
less apportioned cost:	
£50,000 x £30,000 / £150,000	(10,000)
Gain	20,000
Painting	
Proceeds	300,000
less cost	(60,000)
restoration	(50,000)
Gain	190,000

Total gains:	Land	20,000
	Painting	190,000
Total gains		210,000
less annual exempt amount		(3,000)
Amount subject to CGT		207,000

Capital Gains Tax:
£207,000 x 20%   £41,400

6.12

	£
Painting	
Proceeds	20,000
less cost	(5,000)
less restoration	(6,000)
Gain	9,000
Table	
Proceeds	7,800
less costs: (£1,400 + £100)	(1,500)
Provisional Gain	6,300

But gain limited to 5/3 (£7,800 – £6,000) = £3,000.

		£
Total gains:	Painting	9,000
	Table	3,000
		12,000
less annual exempt amount		(3,000)
Amount subject to CGT		9,000

£9,000 x 10% Capital Gains Tax liability   £900.00

6.13

	£
Necklace	
Deemed Proceeds (market value)	8,000
less cost	(5,000)
Gain	3,000

Gain limited to 5/3 (£8,000 – £6,000) = £3,333 – limit does not apply.

Car is an exempt asset.

House is not entirely exempt:

World holiday period counts as deemed occupation under the 'absence for any reason' rule since it is for less than three years and is between periods of actual occupation. Nine months of the final seven years of absence counts as deemed occupation since it was a main residence before this.

The house is therefore exempt for 21.75 years of the 28 years ownership, and chargeable for 6.25 years.

	£
Proceeds	470,000
less cost	(80,000)
Gain	390,000
Exempt £390,000 x 21.75/28	302,946
Chargeable £390,000 x 6.25/28	87,054

	£
Gains Summary:	
Necklace	3,000
House	87,054
Total Gains	90,054
less exempt amount	(3,000)
Taxable	87,054

6.14 The 3,000 rights issue shares (1 for 5 of the total holding of 15,000 shares) acquired in January 2000 will be linked with the original shares from which the rights derive. Therefore the shares will be added into the pool.

The disposal of 14,400 shares in July 2024 will therefore be matched entirely with the shares that are in the pool:

Pool Working:

		Number	Cost £
1/1/1992	Purchase	3,000	9,000
1/1/1999	Purchase	12,000	42,000
		15,000	51,000
1/1/2000	Rights Issue (1 for 5)	3,000	6,000
		18,000	57,000
30/7/2024	Disposal	(14,400)	(45,600)
	Pool balance after disposal	3,600	11,400

Share disposal	£
Proceeds	72,000
less cost	(45,600)
Gain	26,400

Dresser disposal	
Proceeds	6,900
less cost	(3,000)
Gain	3,900
But gain limited to 5/3 (£6,900 – £6,000) =	£1,500

		£
Total gains:	Shares	26,400
	Dresser	1,500
Total gains		27,900
less annual exempt amount		(3,000)
Amount subject to CGT		24,900

Capital Gains Tax

£24,900 x 20%   4,980

6.15 **(1)** The 2,000 shares sold on 15/11/2001 would have been matched against:
- the 1,800 shares bought on 1/12/2001, and
- 200 shares from the FA 1985 pool

(2) The 2,500 shares sold on 15/7/2024 will be matched against the shares in the FA 1985 pool.

(3) *Pool Working:*

		Number	Cost £
1/5/1985	Purchase	1,000	8,000
1/1/1992	Purchase	1,750	15,750
1/1/1995	Purchase	1,500	10,650
		4,250	34,400
15/11/2001	Part Disposal	(200)	(1,619)
		4,050	32,781
15/7/2024	Disposal	(2,500)	(20,235)
	Pool balance	1,550	12,546

Disposal of Shares:

	£	
Proceeds (2,500 x £12)	30,000	
less cost	(20,235)	as above
Gain	9,765	

(4) Computations on other asset disposals:

Land

	£
Proceeds	20,000
less apportioned cost:	
£5,000 x £20,000 / £100,000	(1,000)
Gain	19,000

Antique Brooch

	£
Proceeds	9,600
less cost	(5,500)
Provisional gain	4,100

Gain is limited to 5/3 (£9,600 – £6,000) = £6,000 – limit does not apply.

Antique table

	£
Proceeds	12,000
less cost	(13,500)
Loss	(1,500)

(5)

	£
Gains:	
Shares	9,765
Land	19,000
Antique brooch	4,100
	32,865
less loss on antique table	(1,500)
Net gains	31,365
less annual exempt amount	(3,000)
Amount subject to CGT	28,365
Capital Gains Tax:	
£28,365 x 20% =	£5,673.00

6.16 (a)

Occupation / Deemed Occupation	Non-occupation
1/2/2009 – 31/1/2014	1/2/2014 – 30/9/2023
1/10/2023 – 1/7/2024	

(b)

Total gain calculation:	£
Proceeds	205,000
Cost	70,000
Total gain	135,000

Chargeable gain = £135,000 × (non-occupation period / total ownership period)

= £135,000 × (116 months / 185 months)

= £84,648

6.17

Asset	Sale proceeds	Cost	Statement
1	£4,000	£3,000	Exempt asset
2	£12,000	£8,000	Calculate gain as normal
3	£7,000	£5,000	Chattel marginal relief applies
4	£3,000	£8,000	Sale proceeds to be £6,000
5	£15,000	£21,000	Calculate loss as normal

CHAPTER 7: INHERITANCE TAX

7.1

	£
Inheritance Tax calculation:	
Estate	595,000
less exempt transfer to Sophie	(200,000)
less exempt transfer to political party	(2,000)
less nil rate band	(325,000)
Amount subject to IHT	68,000
Inheritance Tax at 40%	27,200

	£
Calculation of amount received by Jane:	
Estate	595,000
less transfer to Sophie	(200,000)
less transfer to political party	(2,000)
less Inheritance Tax	(27,200)
Balance due to Jane	365,800

7.2 Tony's unused nil rate band will be transferred to Angela. This unused band will be £325,000 − (£20,000 x 3) = £265,000. This is because the transfer on Tony's death to Angela is exempt.

The Inheritance Tax on Angela's death will be calculated as:

	£
Estate	950,000
less residence nil rate band (£175,000 + £175,000)	(350,000)
less nil rate band (£325,000 + £265,000)	(590,000)
Chargeable to IHT	10,000
Inheritance Tax at 40%	4,000

7.3 (a) and (d) are only for lifetime transfers; the others are for lifetime or death transfers.

7.4
- £200 to each of his six grandchildren. These are exempt as each individual receives less than £250 in the tax year.
- A ring worth £5,000 was given to his wife. This is exempt as a gift to his wife.
- A gift of £2,500 was made to a friend who was in financial difficulties. This will be exempt as it is the only gift that falls under the £3,000 annual exemption.
- A gift costing £800 was given to a friend's daughter when she got married. This is exempt, covered by the marriage gifts up to £1,000 by 'anyone else'.
- Sports equipment costing £1,200 was given to a local charity. This is exempt, since all gifts to charity are exempt.

7.5 Inheritance Tax due in lifetime:

The chargeable transfer will not result in any IHT payable immediately, since (after deducting two £3,000 annual exemptions) it is £214,000, which is below the £325,000 threshold.

The gift to Josie is a PET of £25,000, less annual exemption of £3,000 = £22,000. The gift to June is a PET of £25,000.

Inheritance Tax on death:

	£
Estate	720,000
less exempt transfer to wife, Julie	(325,000)
less exempt transfer to political party	(8,000)
less residence nil rate band	(175,000)
less nil rate band	
(£325,000 – £214,000 – £22,000 – £25,000)	(64,000)
Chargeable to IHT	148,000
Inheritance Tax at 40%	59,200

Reference Material

for AAT Assessment of Personal Tax

Finance Act 2024

For assessments from 27 January 2025

Note: this reference material is accessible by candidates during their live computer based assessment for Personal Tax.

This material was current at the time this book was published, but may be subject to change. Readers are advised to check the AAT website or Osborne Books website for any updates.

Introduction

This document comprises data that you may need to consult during your Personal Tax computer-based assessment.

The material can be consulted during the practice and live assessments by using the reference materials section at each task position. It's made available here so you can familiarise yourself with the content before the assessment.

Do not take a print of this document into the exam room with you*.

This document may be changed to reflect periodical updates in the computer-based assessment, so please check you have the most recent version while studying.

This version is based on **Finance Act 2024** and is for use in AAT Q2022 assessments from **27 January 2025**.

*Unless you need a printed version as part of reasonable adjustments for particular needs, in which case you must discuss this with your tutor at least six weeks before the assessment date.

> Note that page numbers refer to those in the original AAT Guidance document

Contents

1.	Tax Rate and bands	4
2.	Allowances	4
3.	Property income allowance	4
4.	Individual savings accounts	4
5.	Deemed domicile	5
6.	Residence	5
7.	Car benefit percentage	6
8.	Car fuel benefit	6
9.	Approved mileage allowance payments (employees and residential landlords)	6
10.	Van benefit charge	7
11.	Other benefits kind	7
12.	HMRC official rate	8
13.	National insurance contributions	8
14.	Capital gains tax	8
15.	Capital gains tax – tax rates	8
16.	Inheritance tax – tax rates	9
17.	Inheritance tax – tapering relief	9
18.	Inheritance tax – exemptions	9

1. Tax Rate and bands

Tax rates	Tax bands	Normal rates %	Dividend rates %
Basic rate	£1 – £37,700	20	8.75
Higher rate	£37,701 – £125,140	40	33.75
Additional rate	£125,141 and over	45	39.35

2. Allowances

	£
Personal allowance	12,570
Savings allowance: Basic rate taxpayer	1,000
Higher rate taxpayer	500
Dividend allowance	500
Income limit for personal allowances*	100,000

* Personal allowances are reduced by £1 for every £2 over the income limit.

3. Property income allowance

	£
Annual limit	1,000

4. Individual savings accounts

	£
Annual limit	20,000

5. Deemed domicile

Deemed domicile	Criteria
Condition A	Was born in the UK
	Domicile of origin was in the UK
	Was resident in the UK for the tax year in question
Condition B	Has been UK resident for at least 15 of the 20 tax years immediately before the relevant tax year

6. Residence

Residence	Criteria
Automatically not resident	Spend fewer than 16 days in the UK (or 46 days if you have not been classed as UK resident for the three previous tax years; or
	Work abroad full time (averaging at least 35 hours a week) and spend less than 91 days in the UK, of which no more than 30 are spent working
Automatically resident	Spend 183 or more days in the UK in the tax year; or
	Only home is in the UK; and
	You owned, rented or lived in the home for at least 91 days and spent at least 30 days there in the tax year.
Resident by number of ties	If UK resident for one or more of the previous three tax years: • 4 ties needed if spend 16-45 days in the UK • 3 ties needed if spend 46-90 days in the UK • 2 ties needed if spend 91-120 days in the UK • 1 tie needed if spend over 120 days in the UK.
	If UK resident in none of the previous three tax years: • 4 ties needed if spend 46-90 days in the UK • 3 ties needed if spend 91-120 days in the UK • 2 ties needed if spend over 120 days in the UK.

7. Car benefit percentage

CO_2 Emissions for petrol engines g/km	Electric range (miles)	%
Nil	NA	2
1 to 50	130 or more	2
1 to 50	70-129	5
1 to 50	40-69	8
1 to 50	30-39	12
1 to 50	Less than 30	14
51 to 54		15
55 or more		16 + 1% for every extra 5g/km above 55g/km
Diesel engines*		Additional 4%

*The additional 4% will not apply to diesel cars which are registered after 1 September 2017 and meet the RDE2 standards.

8. Car fuel benefit

	£
Base figure	27,800

9. Approved mileage allowance payments (employees and residential landlords)

First 10,000 miles	45p per mile
Over 10,000 miles	25p per mile
Additional passengers	5p per mile per passenger
Motorcycles	24p per mile
Bicycles	20p per mile

10. Van benefit charge

	£
Basic charge	3,960
Private fuel charge	757
Benefit charge for zero emission vans	NIL

11. Other benefits in kind

Benefit	Notes
Expensive accommodation limit	£75,000
Health screening	One per year
Incidental overnight expenses: within UK	£5 per night
Incidental overnight expenses: overseas	£10 per night
Job-related accommodation	£Nil
Living expenses where job-related exemption applies	Restricted to 10% of employees net earnings
Loan of assets annual charge	20%
Low-rate or interest free loans	Up to £10,000
Mobile telephones	One per employee
Non-cash gifts from someone other than the employer	£250 per tax year
Non-cash long service award	£50 per year of service
Pay whilst attending a full-time course	£15,480 per academic year
Provision of eye tests and spectacles for DSE (display screen equipment)	£Nil
Provision of parking spaces	£Nil
Provision of workplace childcare	£Nil
Provision of workplace sports facilities	£Nil
Removal and relocation expenses	£8,000
Staff party or event	£150 per head
Staff suggestion scheme	Up to £5,000
Subsidised meals	£Nil
Working from home	£6 per week/£26 per month

12. HMRC official rate

	%
HMRC official rate	2.25

13. National insurance contributions

		%
Class 1 Employee:	Below £12,570	0
	Above £12,570 and below £50,270	8
	£50,270 and above	2
Class 1 Employer:	Below £9,100	0
	£9,100 and above	13.8
Class 1A		13.8

	£
Employment allowance	5,000

14. Capital gains tax

	£
Annual exempt amount	3,000

15. Capital gains tax – tax rates

	%
Basic rate	10
Higher rate	20

16. Inheritance tax – tax rates

	£
Nil rate band	325,000
Additional residence nil-rate band*	175,000

		%
Excess taxable at:	Death rate	40
	Lifetime rate	20

*Applies when a home is passed on death to direct descendants of the deceased after 6 April 2017. Any unused band is transferrable to a spouse or civil partner.

17. Inheritance tax – tapering relief

	% reduction
3 years or less	0
Over 3 years but less than 4 years	20
Over 4 years but less than 5 years	40
Over 5 years but less than 6 years	60
Over 6 years but less than 7 years	80

18. Inheritance tax – exemptions

		£
Small gifts		250 per transferee per tax year
Marriage or civil partnership:	From parent	5,000
	Grandparent	2,500
	One party to the other	2,500
	Others	1,000
Annual exemption		3,000

Reference Material

for AAT Assessment of Personal Tax

Finance Act 2024

Professional conduct in relation to taxation

For assessments from 27 January 2025

Note: this reference material is accessible by candidates during their live computer based assessment for Personal Tax.

This material was current at the time this book was published, but may be subject to change. Readers are advised to check the AAT website or Osborne Books website for any updates.

Reference material for AAT assessment of Personal Tax

Introduction

This document comprises data that you may need to consult during your Personal Tax computer-based assessment.

The material can be consulted during the practice and live assessments by using the reference material section at each task position. It is made available here so you can familiarise yourself with the content before the assessment.

Do not take a print of this document into the exam room with you*.

This document may be changed to reflect periodical updates in the computer-based assessment, so please check you have the most recent version while studying.

This version is based on **Finance Act 2024** and is for use in AAT assessments from **27 January 2025**.

* Unless you need a printed version as part of reasonable adjustments for particular needs, in which case you must discuss this with your tutor at least six weeks before the assessment date.

> Note that page numbers refer to those in the original AAT Guidance document

Contents

1.	Interpretation and abbreviations	4
2.	Fundamental principles	5
3.	PCRT Help sheet A: Submission of tax information and 'Tax filings'	6
4.	PCRT Help sheet B: Tax advice	10
5.	PCRT Help sheet C: Dealing with errors	12
6.	PCRT Help sheet D: Requests for data by HMRC	15

1. Interpretation and abbreviations

Context

Tax advisors operate in a complex business and financial environment. The increasing public focus on the role of taxation in wider society means a greater interest in the actions of tax advisors and their clients.

This guidance, written by the professional bodies for their members working in tax, sets out the hallmarks of a good tax advisor, and in particular the fundamental principles of behaviour that members are expected to follow.

Interpretation

1.1 In this guidance:
- 'Client' includes, where the context requires, 'former client'
- 'Member' (and 'members') includes 'firm' or 'practice' and the staff thereof
- 'Word' in the singular include the plural and 'words' in the plural include the singular.

Abbreviations

1.1 The following abbreviations have been used:

AML	Anti-Money Laundering
CCAB	Consultative Committee of Accountancy Bodies
DOTAS	Disclosure of Tax Avoidance Schemes
GAAP	Generally Accepted Accounting Principles
GAAR	General Anti-Abuse Rule in Finance Act 2013
GDPR	General Data Protection Regulation
HMRC	Her Majesty's Revenue and Customs
MTD	Making Tax Digital
MLRO	Money Laundering Reporting Officer
NCA	National Crime Agency (previously the Serious Organised Crime Agency
POTAS	Promoters of Tax Avoidance Schemes
PCRT	Professional Conduct in Relation to Taxation
SRN	Scheme Reference Number

2. Fundamental principles

Overview of the fundamental principles

1. Ethical behaviour in the tax profession is critical. The work carried out by a member needs to be trusted by society at large as well as by clients and other stakeholders. What a member does reflects not just on themselves but on the profession as a whole.

2. A member must comply with the following fundamental principles:

   Integrity

   To be straightforward and honest in all professional and business relationships.

   Objectivity

   To not allow bias, conflict of interest or undue influence of others to override professional or business judgements.

   Professional competence and due care

   To maintain professional knowledge and skill at the level required to ensure that a client or employer receives competent professional service based on current developments in practice, legislation and techniques and act diligently and in accordance with applicable technical and professional standards.

   Confidentiality

   To respect the confidentiality of information acquired as a result of professional and business relationships and, therefore, not disclose any such information to third parties without proper and specific authority, unless there is a legal or professional right or duty to disclose, nor use the information for the personal advantage of the member or third parties.

   Professional behaviour

   To comply with relevant laws and regulations and avoid any action that discredits the profession.

3. PCRT Help sheet A: Submission of tax information and 'Tax filings'

Definition of filing of tax information and tax filings (filing)

1. For the purposes of this guidance, the term 'filing' includes any online submission of data, online filing or other filing that is prepared on behalf of the client for the purposes of disclosing to any taxing authority details that are to be used in the calculation of tax due by a client or a refund of tax due to the client or for other official purposes. It includes all taxes, NIC and duties.

2. A letter, or online notification, giving details in respect of a filing or as an amendment to a filing including, for example, any voluntary disclosure of an error should be dealt with as if it was a filing.

Making Tax Digital and filing

3. Tax administration systems, including the UK's, are increasingly moving to mandatory digital filing of tax information and returns.

4. Except in exceptional circumstances, a member will explicitly file in their capacity as agent. A member is advised to use the facilities provided for agents and to avoid knowing or using the client's personal access credentials.

5. A member should keep their access credentials safe from unauthorised use and consider periodic change of passwords.

6. A member is recommended to forward suspicious emails to phishing@hmrc.gsi.gov.uk and then delete them. It is also important to avoid clicking on websites or links in suspicious emails, or opening attachments.

7. Firms should have policies on cyber security, AML and GDPR.

Taxpayer's responsibility

8. The taxpayer has primary responsibility to submit correct and complete filings to the best of their knowledge and belief. The final decision as to whether to disclose any issue is that of the client but in relation to your responsibilities see paragraph 12 below.

9. In annual self-assessment returns or returns with short filing periods the filing may include reasonable estimates where necessary.

Member's responsibility

10. A member who prepares a filing on behalf of a client is responsible to the client for the accuracy of the filing based on the information provided.

11. In dealing with HMRC in relation to a client's tax affairs a member should bear in mind their duty of confidentiality to the client and that they are acting as the agent of their client. They have a duty to act in the best interests of their client.

12. A member should act in good faith in dealings with HMRC in accordance with the fundamental principle of integrity. In particular the member should take reasonable care and exercise appropriate professional scepticism when making statements or asserting facts on behalf of a client.

13. Where acting as a tax agent, a member is not required to audit the figures in the books and records provided or verify information provided by a client or by a third party. However, a member should take care not to be associated with the presentation of facts they know or believe to be incorrect or misleading, not to assert tax positions in a tax filing which they consider to have no sustainable basis.

14. When a member is communicating with HMRC, they should consider whether they need to make it clear to what extent they are relying on information which has been supplied by the client or a third party.

Materiality

15. Whether an amount is to be regarded as material depends upon the facts and circumstances of each case.

16. The profits of a trade, profession, vocation or property business should be computed in accordance with GAAP subject to any adjustment required or authorised by law in computing profits for those purposes. This permits a trade, profession, vocation or property business to disregard non-material adjustments in computing its accounting profits.

17. The application of GAAP, and therefore materiality, does not extend beyond the accounting profits. Thus, the accounting concept of materiality cannot be applied when completing tax filings.

18. It should be noted that for certain small businesses an election may be made to use the cash basis instead; for small property businesses the default position is the cash basis. Where the cash basis is used, materiality is not relevant.

Disclosure

19. If a client is unwilling to include in a tax filing the minimum information required by law, the member should follow the guidance in Help sheet C: Dealing with Errors. The paragraphs below (paras 20 – 24) give guidance on some of the more common areas of uncertainty over disclosure.

20. In general, it is likely to be in a client's own interests to ensure that factors relevant to their tax liability are adequately disclosed to HMRC because:
    - their relationship with HMRC is more likely to be on a satisfactory footing if they can demonstrate good faith in their dealings with them. HMRC notes in 'Your Charter' that 'We want to give you a service that is fair, accurate and based on mutual trust and respect'

    - they will reduce the risk of a discovery or further assessment and may reduce exposure to interest and penalties.

21. It may be advisable to consider fuller disclosure than is strictly necessary. Reference to 'The Standards for Tax Planning' in PCRT may be relevant. The factors involved in making this decision include:
    - a filing relies on a valuation
    - the terms of the applicable law
    - the view taken by the member
    - the extent of any doubt that exists
    - the manner in which disclosure is to be made
    - the size and gravity of the item in question.

22. When advocating fuller disclosure than is necessary a member should ensure that their client is adequately aware of the issues involved and their potential implications. Fuller disclosure should only be made with the client's consent.

23. Cases will arise where there is doubt as to the correct treatment of an item of income or expenditure, or the computation of a gain or allowance. In such cases a member ought to consider what additional disclosure, if any, might be necessary. For example, additional disclosure should be considered where:

    - there is inherent doubt as to the correct treatment of an item, for example, expenditure on repairs which might be regarded as capital in whole or part, or the VAT liability of a particular transaction, or

    - HMRC has published its interpretation or has indicated its practice on a point, but the client proposes to adopt a different view, whether or not supported by Counsel's opinion. The member should refer to the guidance on the Veltema case and the paragraph below. See also HMRC guidance.

24. A member who is uncertain whether their client should disclose a particular item or of its treatment should consider taking further advice before reaching a decision. They should use their best endeavours to ensure that the client understands the issues, implications and the proposed course of action. Such a decision may have to be justified at a later date, so the member's files should contain sufficient evidence to support the position taken, including timely notes of discussions with the client and/or with other advisors, copies of any second opinion obtained and the client's final decision. A failure to take reasonable care may result in HMRC imposing a penalty if an error is identified after an enquiry.

Supporting documents

25. For the most part, HMRC does not consider that it is necessary for a taxpayer to provide supporting documentation in order to satisfy the taxpayer's overriding need to make a correct filing. HMRC's view is that, where it is necessary for that purpose, explanatory information should be entered in the 'white space' provided on the filing. However, HMRC does recognise that the taxpayer may wish to supply further details of a particular computation or transaction in order to minimise the risk of a discovery assessment being raised at a later time. Following the uncertainty created by the decision in Veltema, HMRC's guidance can be found in SP1/06 – Self Assessment: Finality and Discovery.

26. Further HMRC guidance says that sending attachments with a tax filing is intended for those cases where the taxpayer 'feels it is crucial to provide additional information to support the filing but for some reason cannot utilise the white space'.

Reliance on HMRC published guidance

27. Whilst it is reasonable in most circumstances to rely on HMRC published guidance, a member should be aware that the Tribunal and the courts will apply the law even if this conflicts with HMRC guidance.

28. Notwithstanding this, if a client has relied on HMRC guidance which is clear and unequivocal and HMRC resiles from any of the terms of the guidance, a Judicial Review claim is a possible route to pursue.

Approval of tax filings

29. The member should advise the client to review their tax filing before it is submitted.

30. The member should draw the client's attention to the responsibility which the client is taking in approving the filing as correct and complete. Attention should be drawn to any judgmental areas or positions reflected in the filing to ensure that the client is aware of these and their implications before they approve the filing.

31. A member should obtain evidence of the client's approval of the filing in electronic or non-electronic form.

4. PCRT Help sheet B: Tax advice

The Standards for Tax Planning

1. The Standards for Tax Planning are critical to any planning undertaken by members. They are:

   - Client Specific

     Tax planning must be specific to the particular client's facts and circumstances. Clients must be alerted to the wider risks and implications of any courses of action.

   - Lawful

     At all times members must act lawfully and with integrity and expect the same from their clients. Tax planning should be based on a realistic assessment of the facts and on a credible view of the law.

     Members should draw their client's attention to where the law is materially uncertain, for example because HMRC is known to take a different view of the law. Members should consider taking further advice appropriate to the risks and circumstances of the particular case, for example where litigation is likely.

   - Disclosure and transparency

     Tax advice must not rely for its effectiveness on HMRC having less than the relevant facts. Any disclosure must fairly represent all relevant facts.

   - Tax planning arrangements

     Members must not create, encourage or promote tax planning arrangements or structures that i) set out to achieve results that are contrary to the clear intention of Parliament in enacting relevant legislation and/or ii) are highly artificial or highly contrived and seek to exploit shortcomings within the relevant legislation.

   - Professional judgement and appropriate documentation

     Applying these requirements to particular client advisory situations requires members to exercise professional judgement on a number of matters. Members should keep notes on a timely basis of the rationale for the judgements exercised in seeking to adhere to these requirements

Guidance

2. The paragraphs below provide guidance for members when considering whether advice complies with the Fundamental Principles and Standards for Tax Planning.

Tax evasion

3. A member should never be knowingly involved in tax evasion, although, of course, it is appropriate to act for a client who is rectifying their affairs.

Tax planning and advice

4. In contrast to tax evasion, tax planning is legal. However, under the Standard members 'must not create, encourage or promote tax planning arrangements that (i) set out to achieve results that are contrary to the clear intention of Parliament in enacting relevant legislation and/or (ii) are highly artificial or highly contrived and seek to exploit shortcomings within the relevant legislation'.

5. Things to consider:
    - have you checked that your engagement letter fully covers the scope of the planning advice?
    - have you taken the Standards for Tax Planning and the Fundamental Principles into account? Is it client specific? Is it lawful? Will all relevant facts be disclosed to HMRC? Is it creating, encouraging, or promoting tax planning contrary to the 4th Standard for Tax Planning?
    - how tax sophisticated is the client?
    - has the client made clear what they wish to achieve by the planning?
    - what are the issues involved with the implementation of the planning?
    - what are the risks associated with the planning and have you warned the client of them? For example:
        - the strength of the legal interpretation relied upon
        - the potential application of the GAAR
        - the implications for the client, including the obligations of the client in relation to their tax return, if the planning requires disclosure under DOTAS or DASVOIT and the potential for an accelerated payment notice or partner payment notice?
        - the reputational risk to the client and the member of the planning in the public arena
        - the stress, cost and wider personal or business implications to the client in the event of a prolonged dispute with HMRC. This may involve unwelcomed publicity, costs, expenses and loss of management time over a significant period

- if the client tenders for government contracts, the potential impact of the proposed tax planning on tendering for and retaining public sector contracts
- the risk of counteraction. This may occur before the planning is completed or potentially there may be retrospective counteraction at a later date
- the risk of challenge by HMRC. Such challenge may relate to the legal interpretation relied upon, but may alternatively relate to the construction of the facts, including the implementation of the planning
- the risk and inherent uncertainty of litigation. The probability of the planning being overturned by the courts if litigated and the potential ultimate downside should the client be unsuccessful
- is a second opinion necessary/advisable?
* are the arrangements in line with any applicable code of conduct or ethical guidelines or stances, for example the Banking Code, and fit and proper tests for charity trustees and pension administrators?
* are you satisfied that the client understands the planning proposed?
* have you documented the advice given and the reasoning behind it?

5. PCRT Help sheet C: Dealing with errors

Introduction

1. For the purposes of this guidance, the term 'error' is intended to include all errors and mistakes whether they were made by the client, the member, HMRC or any other party involved in a client's tax affairs, and whether made innocently or deliberately.

2. During a member's relationship with the client, the member may become aware of possible errors in the client's tax affairs. Unless the client is already aware of the possible error, they should be informed as soon as the member identifies them.

3. Where the error has resulted in the client paying too much tax the member should advise the client to make a repayment claim. The member should advise the client of the time limits to make a claim and have regard to any relevant time limits. The rest of this Help sheet deals with situations where tax may be due to HMRC.

4. Sometimes an error made by HMRC may mean that the client has not paid tax actually due or they have been incorrectly repaid tax. There may be fee costs as a result of correcting such mistakes. A member should bear in mind that, in some circumstances, clients or agents may be able to claim for additional professional costs incurred and compensation from HMRC.

5. A member should act correctly from the outset. A member should keep sufficient appropriate records of discussions and advice and when dealing with errors the member should:
   - give the client appropriate advice
   - if necessary, so long as they continue to act for the client, seek to persuade the client to behave correctly
   - take care not to appear to be assisting a client to plan or commit any criminal offence or to conceal any offence which has been committed
   - in appropriate situations, or where in doubt, discuss the client's situation with a colleague or an independent third party (having due regard to client confidentiality).

6. Once aware of a possible error, a member must bear in mind the legislation on money laundering and the obligations and duties which this places upon them.

7. Where the member may have made the error, the member should consider whether they need to notify their professional indemnity insurers.

8. In any situation where a member has concerns about their own position, they should consider taking specialist legal advice. For example, where a client appears to have used the member to assist in the commissioning of a criminal offence and people could question whether the member had acted honestly in good faith. Note that The Criminal Finances Act 2017 has created new criminal offences of failure to prevent facilitation of tax evasion.

9. The flowchart below summarises the recommended steps a member should take where a possible error arises. It must be read in conjunction with the guidance and commentary that follow it.

Dealing with errors flowchart

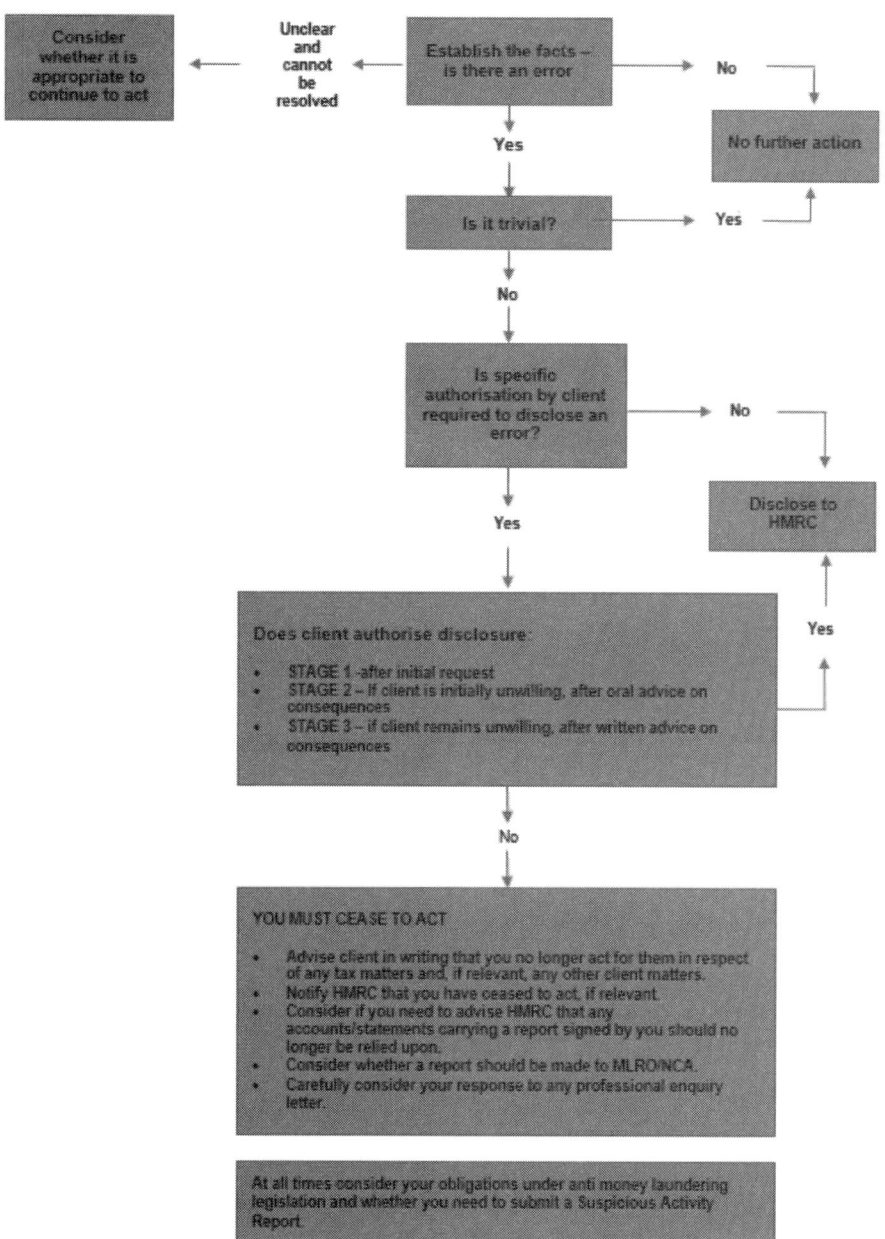

6. PCRT Help sheet D: Requests for data by HMRC

Introduction

1. For the purposes of this help sheet the term 'data' includes documents in whatever form (including electronic) and other information. While this guidance relates to HMRC requests, other government bodies or organisations may also approach the member for data. The same principles apply.

2. A distinction should be drawn between a request for data made informally ('informal requests') and those requests for data which are made in exercise of a power to require the provision of the data requested ('formal requests').

3. Similarly, requests addressed to a client and those addressed to a member require different handling.

4. Where a member no longer acts for a client, the member remains subject to the duty of confidentiality. In relation to informal requests, the member should refer the enquirer either to the former client or if authorised by the client to the new agent. In relation to formal requests addressed to the member, the termination of their professional relationship with the client does not affect the member's duty to comply with that request, where legally required to do so.

5. A member should comply with formal requests and should not seek to frustrate legitimate requests for information. Adopting a constructive approach may help to resolve issues promptly and minimise costs to all parties.

6. Whilst a member should be aware of HMRC's powers it may be appropriate to take specialist advice.

7. Devolved tax authorities have separate powers.

8. Two flowcharts are at the end of this help sheet:
   - requests for data addressed to the member
   - requests for data addressed to the client.

Informal requests addressed to the client

9. From time to time, HMRC chooses to communicate directly with clients rather than with the appointed agent.

10. HMRC has given reassurances that it is working to ensure that initial contact on compliance checks will normally be via the agent and only if the agent does not reply within an appropriate timescale will the contact be directly with the client.

11. When the member assists a client in dealing with such requests from HMRC, the member should advise the client that cooperation with informal requests can provide greater opportunities for the taxpayer to find a pragmatic way to work through the issue at hand with HMRC.

Informal requests addressed to the member

12. Disclosure in response to informal requests can only be made with the client's permission.

13. In many instances, the client will have authorised routine disclosure of relevant data, for example, through the engagement letter. However, if there is any doubt about whether the client has authorised disclosure, the member should ask the client to approve what is to be disclosed.

14. Where an oral enquiry is made by HMRC, a member should consider asking for it to be put in writing so that a response may be agreed with the client.

15. Although there is no obligation to comply with an informal request in whole or in part, a member should advise the client whether it is in the client's best interests to disclose such data, as lack of cooperation may have a direct impact on penalty negotiations post—enquiry.

16. Informal requests may be forerunners to formal requests compelling the disclosure of data. Consequently, it may be sensible to comply with such requests.

Formal requests addressed to the client

17. In advising their client a member should consider whether specialist advice may be needed, for example on such issues as whether the notice has been issued in accordance with the relevant tax legislation and whether the data request is valid.

18. The member should also advise the client about any relevant right of appeal against the formal request if appropriate and of the consequences of a failure to comply.

19. If the notice is legally effective the client is legally obliged to comply with the request.

20. The most common statutory notice issued to clients and third parties by HMRC is under Schedule 36 FA 2008.

Formal requests addressed to the member

21. The same principles apply to formal requests to the member as formal requests to clients.

22. If a formal request is valid it **overrides the member's duty of confidentiality** to their client. The member is therefore obliged to comply with the request. Failure to comply with their legal obligations can expose the member to civil or criminal penalties.

23. In cases where the member is not legally precluded by the terms of the notice from communicating with the client, the member should advise the client of the notice and keep the client informed of progress and developments.

24. The member should ensure that in complying with any notice they do not provide information or data outside the scope of the notice.

25. If a member is faced with a situation in which HMRC is seeking to enforce disclosure by the removal of data, or seeking entrance to inspect business premises occupied by a member in their capacity as an adviser, the member should consider seeking immediate professional advice, to ensure that this is the legally correct course of action.

Privileged data

26. Legal privilege arises under common law and may only be overridden if this is set out in legislation. It protects a party's right to communicate in confidence with a legal adviser. The privilege belongs to the client and not to the member.

27. If a document is privileged: The client cannot be required to make disclosure of that document to HMRC. Another party cannot disclose it (including the member), without the client's express permission.

28. There are two types of legal privilege under common law: legal advice privilege and litigation privilege.

(a) Legal advice privilege

Covers documents passing between a client and their legal adviser prepared for the purposes of obtaining or giving legal advice. However, communications from a tax adviser who is not a practising lawyer will not attract legal advice privilege even if such individuals are giving advice on legal matters such as tax law.

(b) Litigation privilege

Covers data created for the dominant purpose of litigation. Litigation privilege may arise where litigation has not begun but is merely contemplated and may apply to data prepared by non-lawyer advisors (including tax advisors). There are two important limits on litigation privilege. First, it does not arise in respect of non- adversarial proceedings. Second, the documents must be produced for the 'dominant purpose' of litigation.

29. A privilege under Schedule 36 paragraphs 19, (documents relating to the conduct of a pending appeal), 24 and 25 (auditors, and tax advisors' documents) might exist by "quasi-privilege" and if this is the case a tax adviser does not have to provide those documents. Care should be taken as not all data may be privileged.

30. A member who receives a request for data, some of which the member believes may be subject to privilege or 'quasi-privilege', should take independent legal advice on the position, unless expert in this area.

Help sheet D: Flowchart regarding requests for data by HMRC to the Member

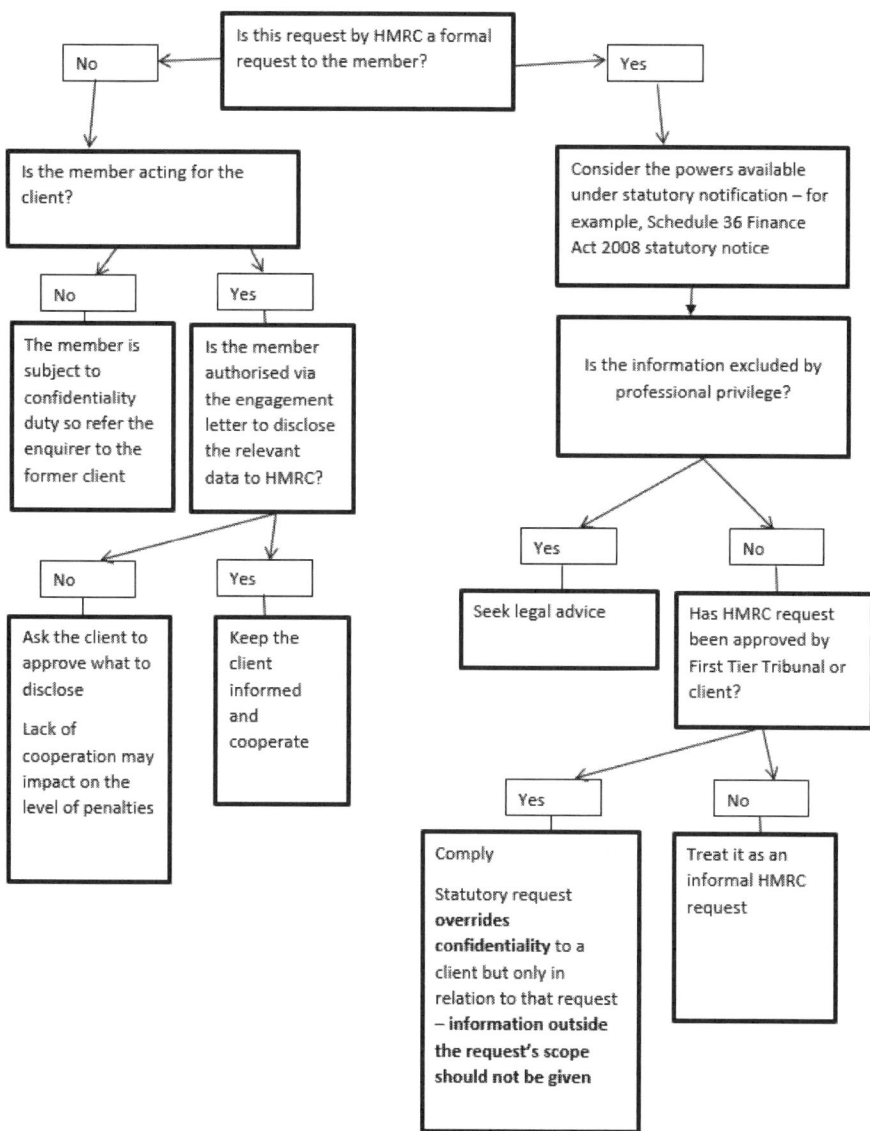

Flowchart regarding requests for data by HMRC to the Client

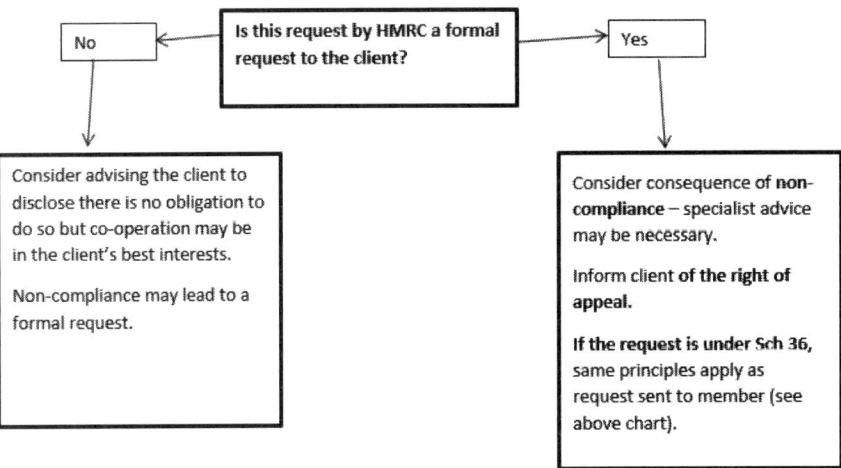

AAT
30 Churchill Place
London E14 5RE

aat.org.uk

AAT is a registered charity. No. 1050724

Index

Accruals basis (property income), 33, 34
Adjusted net income, 108, 112
Allowable deduction, 83
Allowable expenditure against rental income, 35
Allowable expenditure
    Approved Mileage Allowance Payments (AMAP), 84
    entertaining and subsistence, 84
    expenditure reimbursed by the employer, 84
    payroll giving scheme, 85
    pension contributions, 85
    professional fees & subscriptions, 85
    using your own transport, 84
Assessable income, 101

Benefits in kind, 68-83
    beneficial loans, 73-75
    company cars, 69-72
    credit cards, 79
    living accommodation, 75, 76, 77
    provision of other assets, 78
    tax free, 5, 79-81
    trivial, 80-81
    vouchers, 79

Capital expenditure (property income)
    depreciation, 37
    improvements, 37
    renovations, 37
    replacement items, 36
Capital Gains Tax
    annual exemption, 127, 128
    bonus shares, 145
    capital losses, 132, 133
    cars, 126
    chargeable assets, 126
    chattels, 126, 139, 140
    civil partner, 129
    connected person, 129, 130
    disposal, 125, 129
    exempt assets, 126
    FA 1985 pool, 144
    government securities, 126
    improvement expenditure, 136
    incidental costs of acquisition, 130
    losses, 132, 133
    matching rules for shares, 143
    part disposals, 135
    private residence, 126, 136, 138
    rights issue shares, 145
    tax rates and bands, 127
    transfer to 'connected person', 129
    transfer to spouse or civil partner, 129
    wasting chattels, 126, 139
Capital losses, 132
Case law, 8
Cash basis (property income), 33
Cash ISAs, 60
Chattels, 126
Childcare provision, 79
Civil partners, 119, 129, 160
Company cars, 69, 72
    fuel benefit, 72, 73
    pool cars, 73
    scale charge, 69, 73
Confidentiality, 18
Connected person, 129
Contract for services, 67
Credit cards, 79

Deemed domicile, 23
Disposal, 125
   part disposals, 135
Dividend allowance, 53
Dividend income, 51-59
Domicile, 23, 159

Employment income, 67-92
Employment v self employment, 67, 68
Exempt income, 14

Finance Act 1985 pool, 144
Flat rate mileage allowance, 36
Fuel benefit for company cars, 72, 73

Gift Aid, 103, 104
Gifts, 125
Gilts, 126
Government securities, 126

Improvement expenditure (CGT), 136
Income from employment, 67-92
Income from property, 33-42
Income from savings and investments, 51-61
Income Tax
   introduction to, 8
   payment date, 11
   tax bands, 12
Individual Savings Accounts (ISAs), 14, 60
Inheritance Tax, 158-170
   domicile, 159
   chargeable lifetime transfers, 159, 165
   charity gifts at death, 169
   exempt transfers, 159, 160, 164
   lifetime transfers, 164
   overview, 159
   payment, 170
   potentially exempt transfers, 159, 166
   residence nil rate band (RNRB), 162
   tapering relief, 169
   transfers on death, 159, 160, 162
   unused threshold transfers, 162, 163
Investment income, 51-61

Job-related accommodation, 77

Living accommodation, 75-77

Marginal tax rates, 119
Married couples, 119, 129, 160
Mobile telephone provision, 80
Money laundering, 19

National Insurance Contributions, 87-92

Occupational pension scheme, 85

Part disposals, 135
Payroll giving scheme, 85
Pension
   contributions, 85, 104
   personal pension plan, 104
   stakeholder, 104
Personal allowance, 12
   for individuals with high income, 108-109
Personal savings allowance, 52
Pool cars, 73
Principles of taxation, 3-4, 5
Private residence relief (PRR), 136-139
   deemed occupation, 137, 138
Prizes, 14
Progressive tax systems, 5
Property allowance, 36
Property income, 33-42
Property losses, 41
Proportional tax systems, 6

Provision of other assets, 78

Real Driving Emissions Step 2 (RDE2), 71
Redundancy payments, 87
Regressive tax systems, 6
Replacement items allowance, 36
Residence and domicile, 20
Responsibilities of the taxpayer, 16
Responsibilities tax practioner, 18
Rights issue, 145

Savings income, 51-61
Self Employment, 68
Shares
   bonus shares, 145
   matching rules, 143
   rights issue, 145
Staff canteen provision, 79
Statute law, 7
Stocks and shares ISAs, 61

Tax
   avoidance, 17, 18
   band, 12, 52, 127
   computation, 9, 53-59
   direct, 5
   evasion, 17, 18
   indirect, 5
   payment dates, 11, 170
   planning, 17, 117-119
   rates, 12, 52, 102, 109, 160, 165
   structures, 5
   systems, 3
   years, 10
Tax practitioner
   confidentiality, 18, 19
   duties & responsibilities, 18
   money laundering, 19
   professional ethics, 19, 20
Tax-free benefit, 79-80
Tax-free investment income, 59
Taxable income, 8, 11
Transfers on death, 159
Trivial benefits in kind, 80

UK domicile, 20, 23
UK residence, 20-22

Vans, 73
Vouchers, 79

Wasting chattels, 126, 139
Workplace parking, 79

for your notes

for your notes

for your notes

for your notes

for your notes

for your notes

for your notes

for your notes

for your notes

for your notes

for your notes

for your notes